# UNKNOWN SHIPWRECKS AROUND BRITAIN

# UNKNOWN SHIPWRECKS AROUND BRITAIN

## A Diver's Guide

With 16 charts and 6 photographs

**LEO ZANELLI**

KAYE & WARD · LONDON

First published by Kaye & Ward Ltd 1974
Copyright © Kaye & Ward Ltd, 1974

ISBN 0 7182 0963 X

All enquiries and requests relevant to this title
should be sent to the publisher, Kaye & Ward Ltd,
21 New Street, London EC2M 4NT, and not to
the printer.

Printed in England by
Northumberland Press Limited
Gateshead

# INTRODUCTION

This book is the result of the success of my previous wreck book, *Shipwrecks Around Britain*. When I first became aware that *Shipwrecks Around Britain* was fulfilling a need—it is a regular bestseller on the BSAC yearly Book List—it was my intention to write a second book along identical lines, with more wrecks from my files. However it soon became obvious from the many letters I received that the vast majority of readers were most fascinated by the 20% of unknown wrecks in that book.

The reason seems to be that the majority of divers are keen 'wreck detectives'. And it's one thing to dive on a wreck that is well known and documented, but the thrill and satisfaction is much greater if you can name a previously un-named wreck—or discover an entirely new one.

For that reason, this book is composed entirely of either wrecks in which the exact location, but not the name, is known; or the general area of loss of specific, named vessels, in which case the precise site is the unknown element.

I am well aware that in some cases local divers might know the names of some of these 'unknown' wrecks, or the sites of some of the named vessels. Then I can only say that the facts are not on the records of the Hydrographic Department—and they should be. If such people will write in to correct the records, then that alone will justify the effort and time that went into producing this book.

Whether you are a 'diving' wreck detective, or an 'armchair' one browsing through archives, there is enough material here to keep you happy for years. Good luck.

Leo Zanelli

# FOREWORD

I am delighted to receive the opportunity of writing a foreword to this book in particular. Each and every wreck has all the ingredients of a good detective story—except that it is the reader/ diver who has finally to solve the puzzle. And in so doing contribute something tangible towards our limited knowledge regarding these vessels.

I should also like to take this opportunity of pointing out that, although virtually all the unknown wrecks listed here are probably 'modern', there is always the possibility that some of them might prove to be of historical interest, or you might chance upon one that is. If this happens, do not just keep diving on it and/or tell your friends. With the best will in the world, invaluable artifacts or information might be lost for ever. Please, contact an organization such as the Council for Nautical Archaeology, so that the remains can be properly studied and, if necessary, protected. Part of our heritage lies underwater, don't allow what little of it that can be salved to be destroyed or lost.

Alan Bax
*Fort Bovisand Underwater Centre*

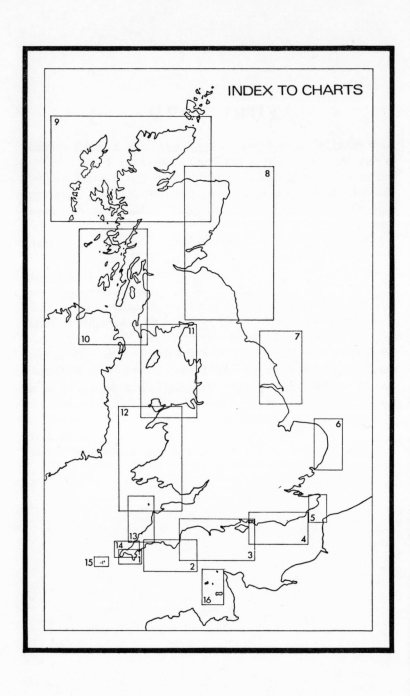

INDEX TO CHARTS

# LIST OF CHARTS

This list of charts and the index to charts on the facing page show how the coastline of the British Isles has been divided into areas. There is a detailed chart of each of these areas in the text, showing the location of the shipwrecks, in close proximity to where details are to be found of the wrecks in the particular chart.

# PHOTOGRAPHS

One of the most difficult tasks in compiling this book has been the location of photographs of 'mystery' vessels. I started with photographs of around fifty ships, only to discover that most of them had been broken up, or wrecked in a distant part of the world, or were still sailing! The problem is that at any period of time there are several vessels of the same name afloat, or that a particular name is one of a series of vessels. The latter system is particularly popular with the Royal Navy, and sometimes a name will have a history running deep into the previous century. The list, eventually, was whittled down to half a dozen vessels, the publishing deadline making it impossible to include any more photographs of vessels that could reasonably be associated with the wreck or ship named. However, I hope you find all of them.

# ACKNOWLEDGEMENTS

I gratefully acknowledge the assistance given me by the Hydrographer of the Royal Navy, Rear Admiral G. P. D. Hall, CB, DSC, and to his Wrecks Officer. And once again, a large portion of the credit must go to Alec Reynolds of the Hydrographic Department, who 'burnt the midnight oil' on my behalf on several occasions.

On the pictorial side, I am indebted to Mr Clarkson, who searched diligently for photographs of some 'mystery' vessels—in fact his superior knowledge prevented me from including a photograph of a 'wreck' that is still afloat!

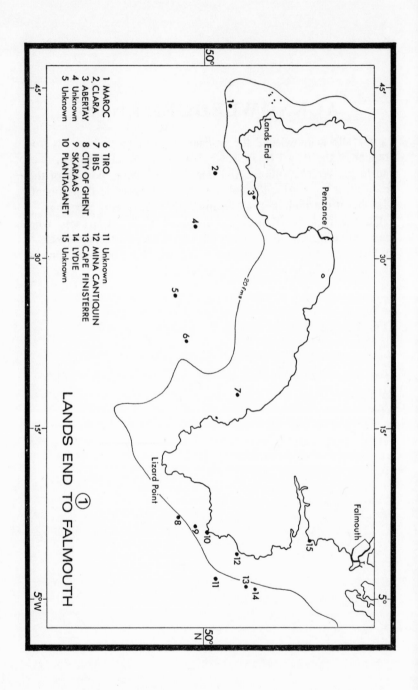

LANDS END TO FALMOUTH ①

1 MAROC
2. CLARA
3 ABERTAY
4 Unknown
5 Unknown

6 TIRO
7 IBIS
8 CITY OF GHENT
9 SKARAAS
10 PLANTAGANET

11 Unknown
12 MINA CANTIQUIN
13 CAPE FINISTERE
14 LYDIE
15 Unknown

## 1. French steamship MAROC

LOCATION: 50° 01′ 30″ N. 05° 43′ 45″ W.

This vessel, 288 tons gross, was built in 1898 by W. Gray & Co., and had dimensions of 306 × 43 × 18·2.

The sinking was caused by a torpedo from an enemy submarine on the 14th April 1918. The position listed is the one given by the master at the time of loss. It is recognized that this is reasonably accurate, and the wreck cannot be too far away because the Maroc went down in only 18 minutes.

## 2. British merchant steamship CLARA

LOCATION: 50° 00′ 38″ N. 05° 37′ 36″ W.

In ballast at the time of loss, the Clara was of 2425 tons gross, 1535 tons net, built in 1897 by Richardson-Duek & Co., of Stockton, and had dimensions of 310 × 44·1 × 20·4. It was owned, at the time, by Buidick & Cook (London).

This vessel was torpedoed by an enemy submarine on the 28th December 1917.

The position is the one given at the time of sinking—which is about 1½ miles SSW of the Runnel Stone. There is an unconfirmed report on the files of the Hydrographic Department that the wreck was located in 1928 by Trinity House, but there is nothing more concrete and Trinity House cannot confirm this.

## 3. French cargo ship ABERTAY

LOCATION: 50° 03′ 00″ N. 05° 35′ 30″ W.

A vessel of 1088 tons gross, built in 1888 by W. Simmons & Co., with dimensions of 221 × 33·1 × 12·9

This French steamer was carrying a cargo of pit props when she went ashore in Boskenna Bay, near Land's End, on the 14th October 1912. The loss occurred near the wreck of another steamer—the South America, which was lost the previous March—so near, in fact, that the crew of the Abertay were able to scramble ashore by climbing over the remains of the South America. First reports indicated that the Abertay, which was slightly offshore, was 'full

1

of water, and salvage is improbable'. Later she was given up and slipped back into deeper water.

## 4. Unknown
LOCATION: 49° 59′ 30″ N. 05° 33′ 00″ W.

This wreck was first located during a survey in 1939, and again in 1944, 1945, and 1954—the last time by Risden Beasley Ltd. The remains are about 240 feet in length, standing some 36 feet high on the sea bed. It has been dived on, but the name of the vessel is still a mystery. One diving group has given the position of the wreck as: 05 *34* 00 W, standing 33 feet high. In view of the fact that all previous surveys confirmed the position given above, it would seem that they either made a mistake in calculation, or there is another wreck nearby.

## 5. Unknown
LOCATION: 49° 58′ 12″ N. 05° 26′ 48″ W.

This is quite a large wreck which stands 20 feet high on the sea bed, and is over 90 feet in length. At a depth of 28 fathoms (168 feet), it is one of the deepest wrecks on this list. There is a probability that this is a World War Two wreck, because, although the area is covered fairly frequently, it was first recorded during a 1941 survey. Further surveys in 1944 and 1945 confirmed the position and details—scant though they are.

## 6. Norwegian steamer TIRO
LOCATION: 49° 58′ 55″ N. 05° 22′ 50″ W.

There is a further mystery about this wreck. It was first discovered in 1918 and, as the location was the one given by the Tiro when she sank, the survey ship assumed that this was the Tiro's site. But although the position has been confirmed, the name of the wreck has not.

Torpedoed by a German submarine on the 29th December 1917, the Tiro was of 1442 tons gross, with dimensions of 234·9 × 37·5 × 15·6, and was built by the Sunderland Shipbuilding Company. At the time of loss, the owners were Christiansen and Poulsen. The depth is approximately 23 fathoms (138 feet).

## 7. Steamship IBIS
LOCATION: 50° 02′ 00″ N. 05° 18′ 00″ W.

Somewhere near this location lies the wreck of the Ibis. On the 12th May 1918, the S.S. Whimbrel was in collision with another vessel, which sank almost immediately. This was at night, and the Whimbrel could not find out the name of the other vessel. However, the body of the 2nd officer of the Ibis was picked up by another ship near this position a few hours afterwards, and the Ibis vanished from that day. So it is pretty certain that this is her graveyard.

At the time of collision, the Whimbrel gave the position as '6 miles NNW of the Lizard', and this is the location listed above. The area is directly out of Gunwalloe, and depths average around 60 feet.

## 8. Irish vessel CITY OF GHENT
LOCATION:    49° 58′ 30″ N. 05° 07′ 15″ W.

This was a vessel of 616 tons gross.

It is a comparatively recent wreck—15th November 1955—and as such would be all the more interesting for any divers who found the remains.

The City of Ghent was on route from Dublin to Fowey at the time of loss. In very low visibility, on a dark evening, she ran aground on some rocks at Penbore, near Black Head. Taking on water rapidly, she then drifted off, in a southerly direction, in a calm sea and with engines out of order. Mayday radio messages were transmitted and a host of rescuers converged on the site—Coastal Command aircraft, the lifeboat, and the M.V. Anteriority. The lifeboat had just transferred the crew of 17 to safety when the distressed ship reached a list of 40°, turned over and sank.

Incredibly, not one of the many vessels at the rescue site bothered to take an accurate fix, so the one given is approximate but reasonably accurate. The City of Ghent now lies somewhere between Black Head and the Lizard, and the depth of water in this vicinity averages over 100 feet.

## 9. SKARAAS
LOCATION:    49° 59′ 30″ N. 05° 06′ 30″ W.

This is quite a large ship, and if ever found should make an interesting dive.

The Skaraas was of 1625 tons gross, was built of steel in 1882, and had dimensions of 259·6 × 34·7 × 19·5.

The sinking was caused by a torpedo from an enemy submarine on the 23rd May 1918. The location given here is very approximate because two rough fixes were given after the loss; the master gave it as '¾ mile SW of Black Head' and another report gives '1 mile SW of Black Head'. At least the reports agree on the direction, if not the distance. One of the reports also states that the vessel sank in 30 seconds—which could indicate that the cargo was very heavy. General sea bed depths are around, or in excess of, 85 feet.

## 10. British steamship PLANTAGENET
LOCATION:  50° 00′ 15″ N. 05° 06′ 00″ W.

Another vessel wrecked off Black Head. The Plantagenet was of 648 tons gross, and built by Alsopp and Sons in 1883. The owners at the time of loss were J. Bacon of Liverpool.

This ship was on route from S. Valerie to Runcorn with a cargo of flints when, in fog, she struck the Struet Rocks, off Black Head, on 20th March 1897. After a while she drifted off and, so contemporary reports say, 'sank in deep water'. This should probably have read 'sank in deeper water', because the approximate area where the Plantagenet went down could hardly be described as deep, although it might be as much as 50 feet—which would no doubt have seemed deep at the time.

## 11. Unknown
LOCATION:  50° 00′ 42″ N. 05° 01′ 42″ W.

This wreck was first located in 1945, and the position was confirmed during a later survey by the Escort Group No. 2. During this second survey, the survey vessel dropped a depth charge over the site. This is sometimes done in case some debris might be removed and drift to the surface, aiding identification. In this case, only some oil was given up. So the mystery remains. Depths in this area touch 150 feet plus, and any attempt at identification would obviously have to be made by experienced divers.

## 12. Spanish coaster MINA CANTIQUIN
LOCATION:  50° 02′ 00″ N. 05° 04′ 00″ W.

This was a compact vessel of 662 tons gross.

The Mina Cantiquin was on route from Newcastle to Join when she struck some rocks off Chynhalls Point at Coverack, on 4th November 1951, in a SW gale. Seriously holed, she drifted for

4

a while, then managed to get the engines going again, but sank off Lowland Point trying to reach shallow water. No lives were lost. The location given is in fact quite close to shore.

### 13. British armed merchant steamship CAPE FINISTERRE
LOCATION: 50° 02′ 30″ N. 05° 01′ 00″ W.

One of the larger vessels on this list, the Cape Finisterre was of 4380 tons gross, and built in 1907 with dimensions of 385 × 49·8 × 18·4.

The loss occurred on the 2nd November 1917, when a torpedo from a German submarine blasted the vessel. The subsequent loss of life was 35, including that of the master.

There is little more on my files about this vessel. The location given is the one at the time of loss, and the stricken ship may have drifted for a while—my records contain no indication of the time the vessel took to sink, which can sometimes add a further clue to the whereabouts. However, a wreck of this size should be well worth looking for. Depths in this area, which is west of the Manacles, are at least 150 feet.

### 14. British armed merchant steamship LYDIE
LOCATION: 50° 03′ 00″ N. 05° 00′ 40″ W.

The Lydie was of 2559 tons gross.

Sunk by a torpedo from a German submarine on the 9th February 1918, with the loss of two lives, there is some confusion as to the final given location of this vessel. At the time of loss, one report gave it as '1 mile E of Manacles Buoy', and the other one as '1 mile E by S of Manacles Buoy'. So, if you are looking for the wreck, you may have to try two slightly different locations. Depths, again, are 150 feet plus.

### 15. Unknown
LOCATION: 50° 06′ 17″ N. 05° 05′ 14″ W.

This wreck lies close inshore, and was first located in 1948. At that time some parts were slightly uncovered at low water springs. The remains are well broken up, but they are dived on from time to time. If anyone finds something that might indicate the name of the wreck, the Hydrographic Department would be grateful to hear of it.

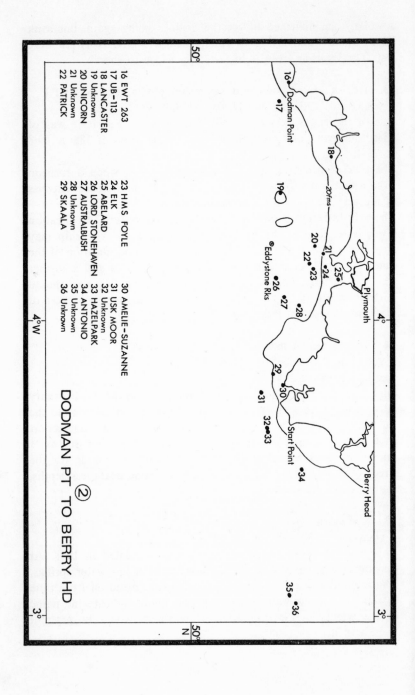

DODMAN PT TO BERRY HD ②

16 EWT 263
17 UB-113
18 LANCASTER
19 Unknown
20 UNICORN
21 Unknown
22 PATRICK

23 H.M.S. FOYLE
24 ELK
25 ABELARD
26 LORD STONEHAVEN
27 AUSTRALBUSH
28 Unknown
29 SKAALA

30 AMELIE-SUZANNE
31 USK MOOR
32 Unknown
33 HAZELPARK
34 ANTONIO
35 Unknown
36 Unknown

Dodman Point
Plymouth
Eddystone Rks
Start Point
Berry Head

### 16. EWT 263
LOCATION: 50° 13′ 24″ N. 04° 48′ 36″ W.

The identity of this wreck has never been confirmed, but it is believed to be that of the 'push barge' EWT 263. This vessel was being towed by a tug, the Britannic, on route from Salamander to Rotterdam, when the tow was broken off Lizard Point. The EWT at this stage started to break up, but was taken in tow again and an attempt was made to take the barge into Falmouth—the after section made it, but the forward section sank, according to witnesses, 'somewhere between Hemerick Beach and Dodman Point'.

### 17. German submarine UB-113
LOCATION: 50° 12′ 00″ N. 04° 45′ 00″ W.

This was a UB-III class submarine with a draught tonnage of 508–650, and dimensions of 182 × 19.

The UB-113 was actually captured and taken in tow at a later date, on route from Harwich to Falmouth. A hawser broke during the tow, and the floating submarine could not be taken into tow again owing to the difficulty of fixing another hawser at sea. It was considered to be a danger to shipping, and HMS Kennet was ordered up to sink the floating hulk by gunfire. HMS Kennet did this very thing on the 14th November 1920—but forgot to take a fix, so the position is approximate.

### 18. LANCASTER
LOCATION: 50° 19′ 06″ N. 04° 33′ 42″ W.

Although this wreck is dived on fairly frequently, little is known about it. It is believed to be a vessel called the Lancaster, which sank on 10th October 1895 after striking Udder Rock. She was carrying a cargo of railway lines, which probably did not help at the time of loss! Because the site is dived regularly, there is a chance that some divers know, or will find out, the name of this vessel, and confirm or refute the name given to it.

### 19. Unknown
LOCATION: 50° 12′ 12″ N. 04° 26′ 12″ W.

This is an intriguing wreck which was first discovered in 1945. At 160 feet, it is a deep wreck for divers, but at 200 feet in length, with a height of 18 feet off the sea bed, an experienced group could find the visit worthwhile.

There is nothing else known, except that the wreck is lying 340°–160°.

## 20. Steamer UNICORN

LOCATION: 50° 16′ 54″ N. 04° 15′ 20″ W.

The name of this wreck, to my knowledge, has never been positively confirmed. This vessel was of 134 tons gross, with dimensions 90·7 × 20·1 × 10·6. The Unicorn was lost on the 9th April 1923, while carrying a cargo of tiles.

The wreck was first located, in September 1971, by Kingston Subaqua Club. According to their findings, the remains are 160 feet in length, although the original vessel would have been about 100 feet (the wreck is broken up), 20 feet wide, lying NE by SW, and 15–20 feet high. There is no deck or superstructure, and the hull is of iron or steel. Because the description fits that of the Unicorn, it is assumed that this is her final resting place.

## 21. Unknown

LOCATION: 50° 18′ 09″ N. 04° 13′ 21″ W.

This wreck was first located during a survey in 1970. There have been no further surveys in this area, so the position has never been confirmed. The site is off Rame Head—a popular diving area—and the depth around 100 feet or less.

A vessel has been wrecked at this location—the steamer Elk—but whether this is in fact the Elk has never been confirmed. An interesting site for further work.

## 22. Trawler PATRICK

LOCATION: 50° 16′ 00″ N. 04° 11′ 36″ W.

This is another wreck which was first located by Kingston Subaqua Club—this time in 1970. It is almost certainly that of the trawler Patrick, which caught fire in the Channel and was gutted. The crew were rescued by helicopter and the Patrick was taken in tow. However the tow was broken and the Patrick sank, on 13th July 1968, in this position. But, even though this wreck has been dived on, there has been no direct evidence as to the name.

## 23. HMS FOYLE

LOCATION: 50° 16′ 38″ N. 04° 10′ 46″ W.

Yet another of the many wrecks located by Kingston Subaqua Club.

Once again, there is some doubt as to the name. From available records, and the general outline of the remains, it could well be HMS Foyle, a small destroyer of 550 tons gross with dimensions 225 × 23·5 × 12. This guess is reinforced by an *unconfirmed* report that some divers recovered a name plate, with the wording Foyle on it, in this area. But I stress that this has never been verified. HMS Foyle was sunk by a mine on the 15th March 1917. The wreck itself is lying on sand, 15 feet high. It is fairly broken up, but intact in one area (not named on my records). There is a 30 degree list, and many pieces of wreckage, including boilers, are lying on the sea bed.

If this is the Foyle, only the stern will be there. After being mined, the Foyle broke in two and the forward section sank somewhere in the Dover Straits. The stern was taken in tow, but sank in this approximate area.

### 24. HM minesweeper ELK
LOCATION: 50° 18′ 00″ N. 04° 11′ 00″ W.

The Elk was a converted trawler of 181 tons gross. On the 27th November 1940, she struck a mine and sank. The last reported position—or rather the last position in which she was seen, because she gave no position—was 185 degrees 11·4 cables from Penlee Point. This is the location given above.

### 25. ABELARD
LOCATION: 50° 19′ 53″ N. 04° 08′ 27″ W.

There is a wreck at this location, and it is believed to be that of the Abelard, a vessel of 187 tons that sank off Plymouth Breakwater on the 24th December 1916.

The position in bearing and distance is (from Plymouth Breakwater Beacon) 2 cables 240 degrees.

The depth over the wreck is about 20 feet.

### 26. HMS LORD STONEHAVEN
LOCATION: 50° 11′ 15″ N. 04° 08′ 24″ W.

The Stonehaven was a requisitioned trawler of 444 tons gross, and was built in 1934. She was torpedoed by an E-boat on the 2nd October 1942, in this approximate location.

At around 150 feet, it's a deep one.

9

### 27. AUSTRALBUSH

LOCATION: 50° 12' 48" N. 04° 04' 52" W.

This is the exact position of a wreck *believed* to be that of the Australbush, a vessel of 4398 tons gross. While on route from Le Havre to Barry, in ballast, the Australbush sank on the 13th November 1917.

The position given at the time of loss was 7½ miles E½N from Eddystone. The Australbush has never been located, but there is a wreck here—and it could be the one. The main problem is that the depth—150 feet—is too deep for all but the most experienced divers.

### 28. Unknown

LOCATION: 50° 14' 42" N. 04° 03' 06" W.

This wreck was first located in 1945, lying at a depth of 125 feet. There are no other details, except that the wreck gave off oil after being depth charged. It could be a rather interesting dive.

### 29. Norwegian steamship SKAALA

LOCATION: 50° 10' 54" N. 03° 49' 06" W.

This wreck was first discovered by a diver in 1970.

It is believed to be that of the Skaala, a vessel of 1129 tons gross, built in 1906, and with dimensions of 229 × 35·2 × 15·9. The Skaala was sunk by a torpedo from a German submarine on the 26th December 1917.

There is precious little information on my files. A diver has reported a wreck in this position, and it is the position given by the Skaala at the time of loss. But until there is positive identification, we can never be quite sure.

The location is off Bolt Head, and is easily reached from Salcombe. The wreck itself, at around 150 feet, is too deep for any but experienced divers.

### 30. Belgian motor fishing vessel AMELIE-SUZANNE

LOCATION: 50° 12' 30" N. 03° 47' 00" W.

This is a comparatively recent loss. The Amelie-Suzanne was lost off Bolt Head, in thick fog, on the 1st April 1972. Although only the approximate location is known, it is reasonably certain that the vessel went down close inshore—this much was gleaned from the crew, who were all rescued.

### 31. British steamship USK MOOR

LOCATION: 50° 09′ 30″ N. 03° 45′ 30″ W.

The Usk Moor was a vessel of 3189 tons gross.

The sinking was caused by a torpedo from a German submarine on the 5th March 1918. In a subsequent report, the master stated that the vessel sank in 10 minutes, so she should not be very far from where she went down. The trouble is, no proper fix was taken at the time of the loss, the location being given as '3 miles SW of Prawle Point'.

Depths in the general area of loss range from 120 feet to 150 feet, so this is no wreck for inexperienced divers to look for.

The nearest site from which to launch a search is Salcombe.

### 32. Unknown

LOCATION: 50° 10′ 24″ N. 03° 37′ 39″ W.

Another deep wreck—this time in 160 feet of water.

The remains were first located during a 1944 survey, but the name of the wreck has never been discovered—probably because of the considerable depth, which limits the site to the expert diver only. Of course, guessing the name of the sunken vessel is part of the fascination of unknown wrecks. In this case, one possibility would seem to be the Hazelpark, which gave this location as the site of sinking. The site is out at sea in between Prawle Point and Start Point. But see Wreck 33 before you make up your mind.

### 33. Armed British merchant steamship HAZELPARK

LOCATION: 50° 10′ 24″ N. 03° 37′ 39″ W.

This, of course, could be Wreck 32, but that is by no means certain. The Hazelpark was a vessel of 1964 tons gross, and was torpedoed by a German submarine on the 20th March 1917. The position given at the time of loss is the one listed above. That is, S by E from Start Point. However, another location given at that time is 50° 10′ 06″ N. 03° 38′ 00″ W.

### 34. British merchant steamship ANTONIO

LOCATION: 50° 15′ 00″ N. 03° 30′ 00″ W.

The Antonio was a vessel of 2652 tons gross, and was mined and sunk directly out from Start Bay on the 9th March 1905. The vessel was built in 1905 by J. Bulmer & Co., and had dimensions of 314 × 46·5 × 28·7.

11

The explosion which sank her also killed the master and crew of 10, so no proper fix was taken.

Depths, again, are considerable in this area—about 150 feet.

### 35. Unknown

LOCATION: 50° 13′ 12″ N. 03° 03′ 58″ W.

This is a real mystery. At least three surveys have verified the position of this wreck since it was first discovered in 1945, but the name is still unknown. Again, this is probably due to the combination of being several miles from the mainland, and in at least 140 feet of water

However, a search should prove interesting because this is no fishing trawler. The wreck stands some 50 feet high on the sea bed (the 140 feet depth mentioned is related from the surface to the top of the wreck); and at this size, must be worth a visit—if you can find it. The wreck lies in a 125–305 degree direction.

### 36. Unknown

LOCATION: 50° 14′ 04″ N. 03° 02′ 37″ W.

This location is near that of Wreck 35, and the fact that the name is still unknown is also probably because of the depth of water and the distance from shore.

The wreck was first located during a 1945 survey. As with the previous wreck, this also is a large vessel. The remains are around 300 feet in length, standing some 38 feet high on the sea bed, which is composed of sand and gravel.

When the wreck was first discovered, the survey vessel carried out the standard procedure of depth charging. As a result of this, the wreck gave off heavy fuel oil, but no items by which it could be identified. So the mystery remains.

### 37. Unknown

LOCATION: 50° 36′ 51″ N. 03° 26′ 28″ W.

By comparison with previous numbers, this is virtually a 'wading' wreck in very shallow water. It is so close to shore that it is incredible that there is no record of any name in the Hydrographic Department.

The wreck was first discovered by a diver in 1964, and the position has been verified by a 1972 report.

The remains stand some 30 feet high (this does not mean that it

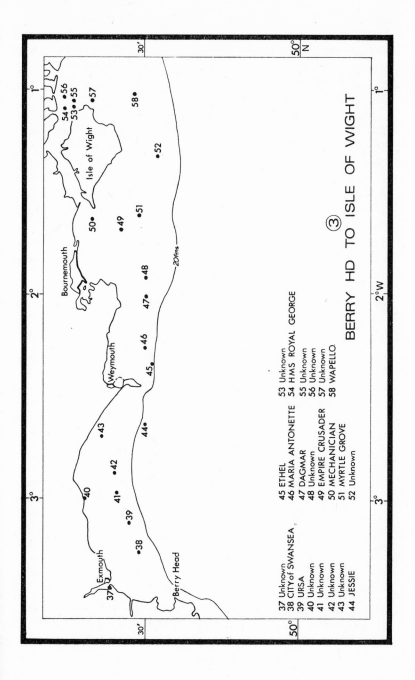

37 Unknown
38 CITY of SWANSEA
39 URSA
40 Unknown
41 Unknown
42 Unknown
43 Unknown
44 JESSIE

45 ETHEL
46 MARIA ANTONETTE
47 DAGMAR
48 Unknown
49 EMPIRE CRUSADER
50 MECHANICIAN
51 MYRTLE GROVE
52 Unknown

53 Unknown
54 HMS ROYAL GEORGE
55 Unknown
56 Unknown
57 Unknown
58 WAPELLO

BERRY HD TO ISLE OF WIGHT

③

was a large vessel—it could be standing on end), with the mast still intact and the hull partly in sand. Both subaqua reports indicate that this could be a small coaster type vessel. Fine, but what name?

### 38.  British merchant steamship CITY OF SWANSEA
LOCATION:    50° 31′ 00″ N. 03° 16′ 00″ W.

The City of Swansea was a vessel of 1375 tons gross, 809 tons net. She was built in 1882, of iron and with one deck, by Palmers of Newcastle, and had dimensions of 260·4 × 35·2 × 16. The owners, at the time of loss, were Belgrave Murphy and Company of Dublin. A torpedo from a German submarine did the damage, and the City of Swansea sank on the 25th September 1917. She was on route to France at the time, and was carrying a cargo of coal.

The site is south of Exmouth and east of Babbacombe Bay. Depths in the general area average about 85 feet—too deep for novices, but a comfortable depth for the qualified club diver.

### 39.  Swedish merchant steamship URSA
LOCATION:    50° 33′ 10″ N. 03° 07′ 15″ W.

The Ursa was a vessel of 1740 tons gross, and 912 tons net. She was built in 1902, of steel and with one deck, by Grangemouth and Greenock. The owner at the time of loss was a Mr B. Ingelsson. Dimensions were 270·3 × 37 × 18·5—large enough to provide a considerable wreck.

While carrying a cargo of coal, the Ursa was torpedoed by a German submarine on the 17th September 1918.

Although several groups have searched for this wreck, which is in an area where the average depth is around 95 feet, it has never, to my knowledge, been found. The location given by the survivors was 'about 7 miles SSW from Beer Head', and this is the location given above. If this is accurate, the Ursa should not be too far away, because reports at that time stated that the vessel sank in 10 minutes.

### 40.  Unknown
LOCATION:    50° 41′ 52″ N. 03° 00′ 12″ W.

This wreck was discovered by a diver—a Mr J. Moore—on the 1st May 1972, when he was diving at Culverhole Point.

Apparently, it appears to be the remains of a steel sailing vessel

14

approximately 100 feet long and 30 feet wide. There are signs that iron ore ballast was carried. The hull itself has been reduced by heavy seas, but the rib structure is still visible, standing, in some parts, 15 feet high.

The location is only about 100 yards offshore, and the tops of the highest ribs are only just covered at low water springs. This should be an easy dive for most clubs and even the relatively novice diver. But finding out the name of the unfortunate vessel requires a great deal of skill and more than a little luck.

### 41. Unknown

LOCATION: 50° 35′ 04″ N. 02° 58′ 42″ W.

First located during a 1945 survey, the position was confirmed in 1972.

The wreck appears to be that of a coaster type vessel about 150 feet in length. Underwater, the bridge can still be made out at the aft end. From above, it gives a good response to echo sounders. The wreck stands some 25 feet high, in about 130 feet of water. The masts have fallen over.

There has been no confirmation as to the name of this wreck, but we can make a guess. This site is the rough position given by a 1544 tons gross vessel, the Marguerite, that was sunk by a torpedo on 28th June 1917. It lies due south of Wreck 40, and should be a good project for the advanced diving section of a subaqua club.

### 42. Unknown

LOCATION: 50° 35′ 04″ N. 02° 58′ 42″ W.

As with the previous four wrecks, this one lies in Lyme Bay. It was first discovered in 1918, and the position was confirmed during a 1952 survey.

The wreck is some 300 feet in length, lying NNE by SSW on a bed of chalk that is covered with fine gravel. Depth is about 90 feet, as is the general area.

Once again, we do not know the name. Several vessels have been recorded as lost in this area, but the one closest to this particular location is that of the Dutch steamship Radaas, a vessel of 252 tons gross that was torpedoed by a German submarine and sank on 21st September 1917. The Radaas has never been located, so this could be it, but until this is confirmed the wreck will continue to be listed as unknown.

### 43. Unknown
LOCATION:   50° 38′ 16″ N. 02° 41′ 56″ W.

This wreck was first located in 1961. It lies in about 90 feet of water and stands some 30 feet above the sea bed. The area it covers is approximately 230 feet by 130 feet lying NE by SW. The remains are heavily corroded, and the vessel is obviously broken athwartships with the stern section highest. It is lying keel uppermost.

What is it? Well, records show that two bucket dredgers have been lost in this approximate location. One was the St Dunstone, which was sunk by a mine on 23rd September 1917, and the other one the Lesrix, about which I have no other information.

It should make an interesting club dive, lying as it does just out from the middle of the Chesil Bank.

### 44. British sailing vessel JESSIE
LOCATION:   50° 30′ 00″ N. 02° 38′ 45″ W.

A rather involved story surrounds the sinking of this vessel. Apparently, the Jessie was captured by a submarine, then sunk by explosives placed on board.

Naturally, during this traumatic experience none of the participants bothered to take a fix. The approximate location given by survivors is '7 miles W½S from Portland Bill'. As this location is some way out at sea, over depths averaging 130 feet or more, the Jessie could remain lost for ever.

### 45. British merchant steamship ETHEL
LOCATION:   50° 28′ 45″ N. 02° 21′ 00″ W.

The Ethel was of 2336 tons gross. She was torpedoed by a German submarine, but did not sink immediately. While still floating, she was taken in tow, but sank shortly after.

This is a good wreck to find out about in winter, because much of the detective work will be research. It should not be too difficult to trace the story and find out the name of the vessel that tried the tow. It is possible that this other ship might have taken a proper fix at the time of sinking. And you would require an accurate fix to search for this wreck, because with this location—south of the Shambles in at least 100 feet of water—the exact site will be difficult to find even if you have a good fix.

### 46. Open trawler MARIA ANTONETTE
LOCATION:   50° 30′ 00″ N. 02° 16′ 00″ W.

This is a comparatively recent wreck, but has not been found at the time of writing. The Maria Antonette sank on 3rd August 1969 after striking a submerged rock, drifting a while, then going down 3–4 miles ESE of the Shambles light vessel. Once again the combination of distance from shore and depth (average about 90 feet for this area) makes it highly unlikely that the remains of this vessel will ever be found, except perhaps accidentally on an echo sounder.

### 47. British steamship DAGMAR
LOCATION: 50° 29′ 40″ N. 02° 00′ 30″ W.
The Dagmar was a vessel of 844 tons. She sank on 9th June 1941, after being bombed by enemy aircraft.
The only location reported is a bearing and distance from St Albans —160 degrees 5¼ miles. This places it in depths in the region of 100 feet.

### 48. Unknown
LOCATION: 50° 29′ 50″ N. 01° 55′ 05″ W.
This wreck was first located during the Second World War by the Escort Group No. 17. The position was subsequently confirmed in 1964.
The wreck itself stands some 25 feet high on the sea bed in a depth of 132 feet. The surrounding bed is of sand and gravel.
Nothing else is known, but it might be worthwhile for an experienced group of divers to make a search because several other wrecks went down in this vicinity.

### 49. Steamship EMPIRE CRUSADER
LOCATION: 50° 34′ 32″ N. 01° 38′ 00″ W.
This was a vessel of 1042 tons gross.
On 8th August 1940, the Empire Crusader was bombed by enemy aircraft and sank '15 miles west of St Catherine's Point, in about 15 fathoms [90 feet] of water'.
The location is not an ideal one. It is on the west side of the Isle of Wight and is exposed to bad seas from the Atlantic. Because of this there are few good diving days each year. But if you happen to be in the area....

### 50. Armed British merchant escort vessel MECHANICAN
LOCATION: 50° 40′ 10″ N. 01° 38′ 00″ W.

The Mechanican was a vessel of 9044 tons gross, with dimensions of 482 × 57 × 31.

The sinking, on 20th January 1918, was caused by torpedoes—two in fact.

At a subsequent court of enquiry, the master stated that he beached the vessel 'on the west side of the west shingle buoy'. A later report, by a survey ship, stated 'It is almost certainly in the position given' (above).

In 1921 the survey ship Flinders attempted to locate the wreck, but without luck. A year later, Trinity House gave the location as 'the south-east edge of the shingle bank in the Needles Channel, with a least depth of 35 feet'.

Records also indicate that salvage attempts were scheduled shortly after the sinking, but I have nothing to indicate that salvage was in fact carried out.

Wreck detectives have many leads to go on. What was the 1921 survey vessel's name, and what was the survey all about? And why was Trinity House so sure of the position a year later? Did Flinders search this exact location? There are many questions to intrigue the curious. A closer look at the transcriptions of the court of enquiry might reveal something.

### 51. British merchant ship MYRTLE GROVE
LOCATION:    50° 31′ 00″ N. 01° 37′ 00″ W.

This casualty was a vessel of 2642 tons gross, 691 tons net, with dimensions of 303 × 41·6 × 19·1. She was built, in 1894, by J. Redhead of South Shields. The owners at the time of loss were Alexander and Main of Glasgow.

The sinking occurred on the 23rd November 1917, as the result of a collision with another vessel. Unfortunately, I do not have the name of the ship that caused the damage.

One report suggests that the Myrtle Grove went down fairly quickly—not surprising, bearing in mind the cargo, which consisted of six railway waggons. There were also 1187 tons of hay on board. Depths, in the region of 90 feet.

### 52. Unknown
LOCATION:    50° 27′ 28″ N. 01° 19′ 54″ W.

This wreck was first located during a 1945 survey. The position was confirmed in 1955. The remains are some 100 feet in length, lying

18

on hard sand at a depth of approximately 120 feet. The position is some way south of the southern end of the Isle of Wight—a location that would require a boat, finding equipment, and an experienced team of divers in a well organized expedition. But it could be worth the effort.

## 53. Unknown
LOCATION: 50° 43′ 55″ N. 01° 05′ 21″ W.
This wreck was first located during a 1950 survey. The position was confirmed in 1972. The remains seem to be in two parts, one of them around 220 feet in length, and standing some eight feet high, on a bed of mud, in general depths of 26 feet. It is lying in a 155 × 335 degree direction.
Horizontal sextant fixes are: 75° 50′ from Yarborough Monument to All Saint's Church at Ryde, 88° 15′ to Portsmouth Power Station north chimney.
The position is relatively sheltered from SW winds, and should be worth a visit at slack tide.

## 54. HMS ROYAL GEORGE
LOCATION: 50° 45′ 26″ N. 01° 06′ 45″ W.
This wreck is outside the general scope of this book, but is included because of its historical interest.
The Royal George foundered at Spithead on 29th August 1782, in the approximate position given above.
During 1841–3, dispersal operations were carried out on the wreck—according to the records, at this very position. The Hydrographic Department holds records of these operations.
There is a wealth of literature documenting the sinking of this vessel, so it would be pointless repeating the details here.

## 55. Unknown
LOCATION: 50° 43′ 48″ N. 01° 03′ 38″ W.
Two survey ships, in 1962 and 1972, located and confirmed the position of this wreck.
The remains stand some 12 feet high, in general depths of 97 feet. There is a small 2-foot scour at one side.
Horizontal sextant fixes are: St Helen's Fort Lantern 84° 51′ to No Man's Land Fort Lantern, 43° 23′ to Portsmouth Power Station north chimney.

This and Wreck 54 both lie in shipping channels in water of rather poor visibility, so good planning and extreme caution are essential to the safety of any expedition.

### 56. Unknown
LOCATION: 50° 45′ 43″ N. 01° 02′ 12″ W.
This wreck was located by a subaqua diver in 1969.
The report states that a 'very unusual object' was discovered. On further investigation it was found to be of iron construction, very old, and mostly rusted away. The general shape is that of a framework with dimensions of 25 × 6 × 5 (last dimension is height), and covered with weed.
What is it? A ship? Pontoon? It is not too far out, and must be worth a visit, if only to clear up the questions.

### 57. Unknown
LOCATION: 50° 40′ 06″ N. 01° 03′ 15″ W.
This wreck was first located during a 1963 survey, and the position was confirmed in 1972.
The various reports state that the remains are fairly old and overgrown with shells and weed. The wreck has probably rolled over, and is now lying in a gulley in the sea bed. It stands some 13 feet high in general depths of 38 feet. The wreckage covers an area of approximately 180 × 30 feet.
Horizontal sextant fixes are: Yarborough Mast 70° 15′ to Bembridge Lifeboat Station at the east corner, 113° 58′ to the Nab Television Mast.
What is it? Records show that the France Aimée, a French cargo steamship of 699 tons gross, sank in this approximate location on 3rd April 1918, carrying a cargo of coal. If this is not her grave —and the area of wreckage would seem to argue to the contrary— then what is the name of this wreck? And where is the France Aimée?

### 58. WAPELLO
LOCATION: 50° 31′ 53″ N. 01° 01′ 07″ W.
The Wapello was a vessel of 5576 tons gross. Available records state that she was sunk by a torpedo from an enemy submarine on 15th June 1917, about 14 miles WSW from the Owers Light Vessel. Nothing else is known.

1. H.M.S. Blackwater, lost on 6 April 1903 after a collision with the steamship Hero. (*Imperial War Museum*)

2. This vessel is named the Calcium. The photograph was taken at Fleetwood in the late 1920s. Is this Wreck 203? (*John Clarkson*)

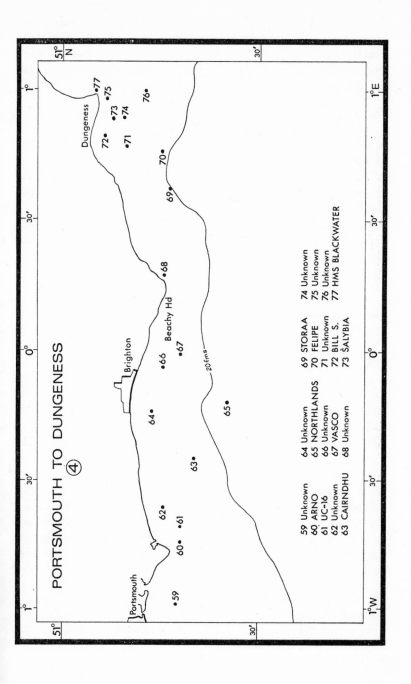

PORTSMOUTH TO DUNGENESS ④

Portsmouth
Brighton
Beachy Hd
Dungeness

20 fms

59 Unknown
60 ARNO
61 UC-16
62 Unknown
63 CAIRNDHU

64 Unknown
65 NORTHLANDS
66 Unknown
67 VASCO
68 Unknown

69 STORAA
70 FELIPE
71 Unknown
72 BILL S.
73 SALYBIA

74 Unknown
75 Unknown
76 Unknown
77 HMS BLACKWATER

The size of the Wapello means that the wreck would certainly be of interest to salvage companies—if they can find out where it is. One of the problems here is that the position is an exposed one. You could be in the area for a fortnight and not obtain one good day for diving.

### 59. Unknown
LOCATION: 50° 42' 47" N. 00° 59' 33" W.

A 1957 survey first located this wreck, and the position was subsequently confirmed during further surveys in 1964, 1970, 1971.

All reports indicate that it could be a small vessel, standing some 15 feet high in general depths of 60 feet. As the site lies directly out from Portsmouth, there should be no difficulty for an enterprising group to dive there, and perhaps give a name to the remains. Horizontal sextant fixes are: Yarborough Monument 65° 52' to Horse Sand Fort Light, 102° 07' to Cackeham Tower.

### 60. British steam collier ARNO
LOCATION: 50° 42' 00" N. 00° 45' 00" W.

The Arno was of 1089 tons gross, with dimensions of 232·1 × 30·1 × 17·1. She was built in 1871.

The wrecking occurred on 11th February 1899, the records indicating 'near Selsey Bill'. The cargo was probably coal.

It is an old wreck, and the relatively shallow depths (about 25 feet) should mean that heavy seas over the years have broken the remains up. But it should be worth a search by a keen subaqua club.

After the sinking, a Board of Trade inquiry was held at Sunderland. The findings, briefly, were that the Arno, owned by Mr James Westoll of Sunderland, foundered near Selsey Bill on route from the Tyne to Peorsmouth. 13 lives were lost. 4 people survived; Captain James Lockland Stansfield, the carpenter and two seamen. The Court found that the vessel was not navigated with proper and seamanlike care, and that its loss was caused 'by the default of the master'. Captain Stansfield's certificate was suspended for three months.

### 61. German submarine UC-16
LOCATION: 50° 42' 00" N. 00° 41' 00" W.

This submarine was of 400/511 tons displacement, 162 feet in length, and with a 17 foot beam.

According to records, the UC-16 was located by the destroyer Melampus, chased, and sunk with depth charges. The Melampus is quite certain that the UC-16 was in fact sunk because of oil and debris that surfaced after the explosions. However, the destroyer unfortunately failed to take an accurate fix at the time.

### 62. Unknown
LOCATION:  50° 44′ 41″ N. 00° 36′ 48″ W.
This wreck was discovered when a 1970 survey ship reported 'a three fathom obstruction'. A subsequent survey, in 1972, confirmed the position.
The location, within easy reach of Bognor Regis and Littlehampton, should present no problem to any diver. Apparently, local fishermen have regarded this obstruction as a submerged group of rocks, but this has never been established—it could quite easily be a wreck.

### 63. Armed British merchant steamship CAIRNDHU
LOCATION:  50° 40′ 00″ N. 00° 25′ 00″ W.
The Cairndhu was a substantial vessel of 4019 tons gross, with dimensions of 370 × 51 × 24·6. She was built by W. Doxford and Sons in 1911, and was owned, at the time of loss, by Cairns Noble and Co.
On route from the Tyne to Gibraltar with a cargo of coal, the vessel was struck by a torpedo on 15th April 1917 and sank 'west of Beach Head'. The captain survived, but 11 of the crew were lost. No accurate fix was taken at the time, and the above location is an approximation.

### 64. Unknown
LOCATION:  50° 46′ 21″ N. 00° 14′ 00″ W.
This wreck was first located by a subaqua club in 1970, who reported 'A 4-engined bomber, upside down, with 2 very large wheels and one wing. All the engines are there, and the remains stand 8 feet high'.
The location was subsequently confirmed by a RN survey ship, and is a short way out from Hove.
There is a current vogue among subaqua clubs to raise aircraft for museums. Part of this enthusiasm is no doubt due to the fact that aircraft, while substantial items, are still small enough to be lifted with a relatively small amount of lifting gear. Anyway, if you

23

fancy a dive on a wrecked aircraft, get in quick—if it's still there!

## 65. British merchant ship NORTHLANDS
LOCATION:   50° 35′ 00″ N. 00° 12′ 00″ W.

This vessel, of 2776 tons gross, was torpedoed by a German submarine 'SW from Beach Head', and sank on 5th April 1915.

Any search for the Northlands will have to be made, initially, with sounding equipment and, if found, dived only by experienced divers because the depths in the area exceed 120 feet.

The sinking of the Northlands, owned by the Northlands Steamship Co., and built in 1900, is well documented. On route from Tunis to Middlesborough with a cargo of iron ore, she was approached by a German submarine which surfaced and drew alongside. The submarine called out for the crew to abandon ship, and when the boats were pulling clear, torpedoed the Northlands which soon sank.

At the time it was stated that the submarine was the U-12. However, a recent Admiralty statement indicates that the U-12 had been rammed and sunk earlier. There is a possibility that the submarine could have been the U-20.

## 66. Unknown
LOCATION:   50° 44′ 45″ N. 00° 03′ 45″ W.

This wreck was first discovered during a survey in 1912, when it was reported as being '5½ miles SSE from Brighton West Pier'. In 1936, the RN swept the area down to a depth of 60 feet, but did not locate the obstruction. However, this does not mean that the first survey made a mistake, because the depths in this area average around 75 feet. And in any case, the wreck would probably have collapsed in the ensuing years. There is very little doubt that there is a wreck in this area, and it could be very old. It must be worth a visit.

## 67. Armed British merchant steamship VASCO
LOCATION:   50° 42′ 00″ N. 00° 01′ 00″ W.

This was a vessel of 1914 tons gross, with dimensions of 280 × 40 × 19·2 and was built in 1895 by Furness Withy and Co.

The Vasco struck a mine and sank on 16th November 1916. All the crew—17 of them—were lost.

No fix was given at the time of loss, but reports stated that the sinking occurred 'approximately ten miles W by S from Beachy Head'. This of course is an enormous area to cover, and it is highly unlikely that the Vasco will ever be found. Having said that, someone is sure to write to me and say that they have been diving on it for years! Depths in the area average around 75 feet.

## 68. Unknown
LOCATION: 50° 44′ 40·6″ N. 00° 17′ 12·5″ E.

This wreck was first located by a subaqua diver in 1970. He stated that it seemed to be 'an old steel ship which appears to have been blown up some time ago. The wreckage is strewn over a 150 feet radius, and stands some 8 feet high in general depths of 16 feet.'

This should be an easy one, even for novice divers, because of the relatively shallow depth and the proximity to shore. However, care should be taken as the tide does flow quite fast at times past Beachy Head.

## 69. STORAA
LOCATION: 50° 43′ 39″ N. 00° 37′ 18″ E.

The Storaa was formerly a Danish steamship which was taken over by Britain on the occupation of Denmark by the Germans in 1940. She had been scuttled at the port of Lyautey, but was raised and repaired in January 1943. Subsequently, she was torpedoed by an E-boat on 3rd November 1943.

Built in 1918 by Greenock and Grangemouth Dockyard Co., the Storaa was of 1967 tons gross with dimensions of 281·6 × 41·9 × 18·6.

The site of the sinking is out at sea about halfway between Beachy Head and Dungeness, on the 20 fathom (120 feet) line. This is too deep for the club diver, but the wreck could just as easily be inside the line, in shallower water, as outside it.

## 70. Spanish steamship FELIPE
LOCATION: 50° 45′ 00″ N. 00° 46′ 00″ E.

Built in 1888, by R. Dixon and Co., and owned at the time of loss by Vivda de F. Astorqui, the Felipe was a vessel of 2204 tons gross with dimensions of 275 × 37 × 19.

On route from Rotterdam to Cadiz with a cargo of coal, she sank, after a collision with another ship, on 3rd September 1926.

The reported area of loss is just inside the 20 fathom line, and there is every chance that the wreck resides in a relatively diveable depth—but first you have to find it!

A newspaper report—*The Times*, I think—printed this message by the British steamship El Uruguayo: 'Been in collision with the Spanish Felipe of Bilbao. The Felipe sank, but the crew have been saved. The El Uruguayo, as far as we can see, has only slight damage. We are proceeding to Rotterdam.'

There is a possibility that the El Uruguayo eventually submitted a fuller report, now in some archive. And it may contain a more exact fix than the approximation given above.

### 71. Unknown

LOCATION: 50° 50′ 14″ N. 00° 46′ 57″ E.

This wreck was first reported during a 1918 survey. Several subsequent surveys have confirmed the position.

The latest report states that the wreck lies in 75 feet of water, on its side, and that the least depth over the wreck is some 45 feet. This means that the wreck stands some 30 feet high on the sea bed—a considerable height indicating a large wreck. It lies off Rye Bay, and because of its size should not be too difficult to find; it should also provide a very worthwhile dive. It is surprising that it has not been dived on before. Perhaps it has, but there are no reports to this effect held by the Hydrographic Department.

Horizontal sextant fixes are: Congregational Church 80° 41′ to beacon red flashing light at the entrance to Rye Harbour, 60° 02′ to Dungeness Lighthouse. The location is also given as: 237½° 8·43 miles from Dungeness Lighthouse.

### 72. Dutch motor vessel BILL S

LOCATION: 50° 53′ 42″ N. 00° 49′ 24″ E.

The Bill S, of 466 tons gross, was bombed and sunk on 10th July 1940 while carrying a cargo of cement.

There is no accurate fix available, but three different reports from that period give a location of sorts. Unfortunately, they all differ. They are: 260° 6 miles, or 55° 5 miles, or 67° 6–7 miles—all from Dungeness.

There are no records available of the wreck ever being worked on by a salvage company, so it should still be substantially around.

One thing is certain—with that sort of cargo it would not have drifted far before sinking.

### 73. British merchant steamship SALYBIA
LOCATION:   50° 52′ 30″ N. 00° 53′ 30″ E.
Very little is known about this vessel of 3352 tons. She was torpedoed and sunk on 24th March 1916, '4 miles SW by W from Dungeness'.

### 74. Unknown
LOCATION:   50° 50′ 50″ N. 00° 53′ 33″ E.
First located during a 1970 survey, this wreck stands some 30 feet high in general depths of 112 feet.
The area was searched by a survey ship after a local trawler reported a fouled net. An echo trace indicated that it was lying NE by SW, and is about 350 feet in length.
The local coastguard say that this wreck is known locally as the 'bottle ship', because of the many bottles that were swept ashore after sinking. The trouble is, no one seems to remember the date of sinking. However, a crawl through the local pubs might locate someone who does.

### 75. Unknown
LOCATION:   50° 53′ 09″ N. 00° 58′ 06″ E.
First located in 1970, when a survey ship recorded the location, and the wreck at a least depth of 14 fathoms. A subsequent visit confirmed the location and stated that the wreck is upside down, and stands some 30 feet high in general depths of 115 feet.

### 76. Unknown
LOCATION:   50° 47′ 32″ N. 00° 59′ 48″ E.
This wreck was first located in 1971. Echo traces indicate that it is at least 15 feet high on the sea bed, in general depths of 102 feet. It lies SW by NE, and is about 120 feet in length.
Although the position is several miles south of Dungeness, it is well within reach of a good boat dive, and as such should be well worth a visit.

### 77. HMS BLACKWATER
LOCATION:   50° 55′ 00″ N. 01° 00′ 00″ E.

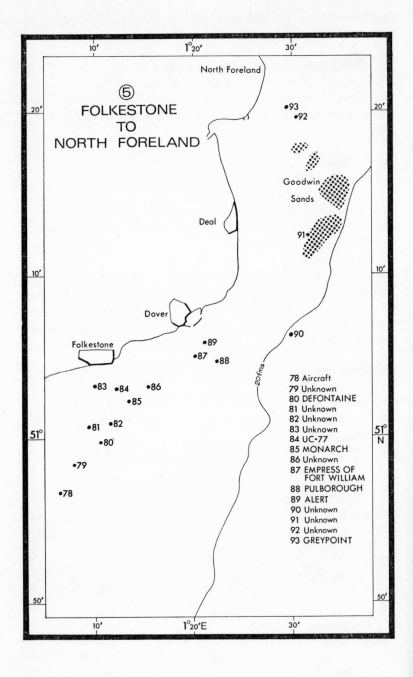

⑤
FOLKESTONE
TO
NORTH FORELAND

North Foreland

Deal

Goodwin
Sands

Dover

Folkestone

78 Aircraft
79 Unknown
80 DEFONTAINE
81 Unknown
82 Unknown
83 Unknown
84 UC-77
85 MONARCH
86 Unknown
87 EMPRESS OF
   FORT WILLIAM
88 PULBOROUGH
89 ALERT
90 Unknown
91 Unknown
92 Unknown
93 GREYPOINT

Blackwater was a destroyer of 550 tons displacement, with dimensions of 225 × 23, and was built in 1903.

The sinking occurred on 6th April 1909, after a collision with the steamship Hero. There were no casualties.

No official position was given at the time of loss, so the above location is approximate.

## 78. Beagle aircraft G-ASAD

LOCATION:    50° 56′ 30″ N. 01° 06′ 24″ E.

On the 30th August 1970, a 3-seater beagle with registration markings G-ASAD was reported as having crashed into the sea, in 90 feet of water, off Dungeness Light.

Despite its 'newness', this should make a good dive for aircraft fans—if they can find it.

## 79. Unknown

LOCATION:    50° 58′ 20″ N. 01° 07′ 51″ E.

This wreck was first located during a 1940 survey. The position has been confirmed by subsequent surveys.

Reports indicate that the remains stand some 20 feet high on the sea bed, in general depths of 90 feet. There is a scour, some 3 feet deep, by the side, and the wreck is 'fairly large'.

This one must be worth a visit. The location has been confirmed several times, boats are available from nearby Folkestone, and the wreck is large. What more do you need?

## 80. British steamship DEFONTAINE

LOCATION:    50° 59′ 45″ N. 01° 10′ 10″ E.

This vessel was of 1721 tons gross, 1063 tons net, with dimensions of 268·2 × 37·7 × 17, and was built, in 1901, by S. P. Austin and Sons of Sunderland.

She was sunk by a mine on 16th November 1918, while in ballast. The position is in the middle of an area that, on most charts, is marked 'Numerous sunken wrecks'. And with good reason. So if you do not find the Defontaine you might bump into one of the others. General sea bed depths are around 80 feet.

## 81. Unknown

LOCATION:    50° 00′ 47″ N. 01° 09′ 02″ E.

This wreck was first located in 1915, and is presumed to be a World War One loss.

According to echo traces, the wreck is lying on its side, and stands about 33 feet high on the sea bed in general depths of 81 feet. This is certainly a considerable height for a vessel on its side, and indicates a large wreck.

Horizontal sextant fixes are: Littlestone Tower 79° 12′ to Tolsford Mast, 55° 40′ to Hungham Mast. This is almost due south of Folkestone.

### 82. Unknown
LOCATION: 51° 00′ 56″ N. 01° 11′ 15″ E.

This wreck was first located during a survey in 1949. Subsequent surveys have confirmed the position.

It stands about 27 feet high, in general depths of 75 feet, and there is a small 4-foot scour at the side.

That's about all. Unless it is standing on end, the height would seem to indicate that it is a substantial wreck, well worth a visit.

### 83. Unknown
LOCATION: 51° 03′ 03″ N. 01° 09′ 57″ E.

This 'wreck' was first reported in 1960, and subsequent surveys have confirmed the location—but not the object. The 1960 report stated that they had found a 'wreck at a depth of 70 feet, standing some 11 feet high'. The second report, however, stated that 'it may be a rock'. Other reports merely state that it is 'an object on the sea bed'.

So we have two mysteries. First, is it a wreck? And if it is, what wreck is it? The location is not far out from Folkestone, so it should not be too difficult to check.

### 84. German submarine UC-77
LOCATION: 51° 03′ 00″ N. 01° 12′ 00″ E.

The UC-77 was a World War One casualty. It was originally sighted on the surface of the water, dived, but was depth charged and sank on 10th August 1918.

According to records, the surface displacement was of 400 tons, and the underwater displacement of 511 tons, with a length of between 162 to 173 feet and a beam of 17 feet.

As with most sinkings of this type, the affair was a hurried, traumatic job, and no accurate fixes were taken, so the above position is an approximation.

### 85. Cable laying vessel MONARCH
LOCATION: 51° 02′ 15″ N. 01° 13′ 30″ E.
The Monarch (this is a common name for cable laying vessels; does anyone know why?) was a vessel of 1122 tons gross, 752 tons net, with dimensions of 240 × 33 × 12·9. Built of iron, with one deck, by David J. Dunlop of Port Glasgow in 1883, she was owned by the Telegraph Department of HM Postmaster General. The sinking occurred after striking a mine on 8th September 1915.
The position is relatively near Folkestone—and if you take this route you will probably pass over the German submarine UC-77 (Wreck 84) on the way.

### 86. Unknown
LOCATION: 51° 03′ 03″ N. 01° 15′ 20″ E.
This is a fairly large wreck, first located in 1960. It stands some 17 feet high on the sea bed in general depths of 87 feet. There is a 7-foot scour at the side.
What is it? Only some divers could tell us this. However, the armchair wreck detective could hazard a few guesses. Several wrecks are known to reside in this approximate area. It could, for example, be the German submarine UC-77. Unlikely, though, because it is quite a distance from the reported position. But bear in mind that the position given for the UC-77 was very approximate. And on this reckoning, it could even be the Empress of Fort William (Wreck 87).

### 87. British merchant steamship EMPRESS OF FORT WILLIAM
LOCATION: 51° 05′ 00″ N. 01° 20′ 00″ E.
This vessel, of 2181 tons gross, is one of a family of a great shipping line. As such, it would be a waste of time quoting specifications here; detailed ones can easily be obtained from the company.
The only thing known about the sinking is that the Empress was mined 'about 2 miles south of Dover Pier' on 27th February 1916. I have heard that the wreck has been dived on—even that salvage work has been carried out—but there is nothing positive about this in my records, or those of the Hydrographic Department.

**88. Steamship PULBOROUGH**
  LOCATION:   51° 04′ 39″ N. 01° 22′ 06″ E.
A World War Two casualty, the Pulborough, of 960 tons gross, was bombed by enemy aircraft and sunk on 20th July 1940. The location—an approximation—was given as '2½ miles SE by S from Dover Pier'.
Nothing else pertaining to this vessel is on my files.

**89.   Trinity House yacht ALERT**
  LOCATION:   51° 06′ 00″ N. 01° 21′ 00″ E.
The Alert, of 777 tons gross and with dimensions of 198 × 32·1 × 12·5, was built in 1911. She was mined and sunk 'off Dover' on 15th April 1917.
A glance at chart 5 will show that I have listed three 'exact position unknown' wrecks (87-88-89) in one area. There are more. A speculative survey of the area could prove worthwhile.
Depths in the area are about 90 feet in general.

**90.   Unknown**
  LOCATION:   51° 06′ 20″ N. 01° 29′ 45″ E.
This is a fairly large wreck, first located during a survey in 1960. It is a deep one, for experienced divers only, standing some 25 feet high in general depths of 165 feet. There is a small scour at one side and the bed is smooth and sloping.
Successive surveys since 1960 have confirmed the position, and horizontal sextant fixes are: Folkestone Breakwater 30° 17′ to South Foreland Lighthouse, 26° 49′ to Parker's Cup.
I cannot stress too strongly that only a well organized expedition of well trained divers should even attempt this dive. In addition to the great depth, the scour at the side of the wreck indicates a considerable current at the bottom.

**91.   Unknown**
  LOCATION:   51° 12′ 22″ N. 01° 31′ 24″ E.
You could almost walk on this one! A mast is invariably visible at high water, although at one time there were four masts showing. It is surprising that the name of such a wreck could remain unknown, but then, the Goodwin Sands are not exactly popular with the subaqua diver because of the treacherous sands, unpredictable weather conditions and poor underwater visibility. If you want

to try this one, pick a period of settled weather and dive at high water when there should be at least 2·5 metres of mast sticking out of the water.

## 92. Unknown

LOCATION:    51° 19′ 38″ N. 01° 30′ 48″ E.

Some distance to the north of the Goodwin Sands, this wreck was first located in 1950, and the position has subsequently been confirmed. It stands some 7 feet high in general depths of 35 feet, and there is a small scour at the side.

As an additional aid to location, horizontal sextant fixes are: South-east chimney of hotel 41° 32′ to Ramsgate Church Spire, 44° 47′ to North Foreland Light.

An interesting thought; could this in fact be the Greypoint (Wreck 93)? Possibly not, because that vessel was sunk in 1917, and it is unlikely that it would have remained undiscovered for 33 years in such shallow water. But we cannot be sure.

## 93. British merchant steamship GREYPOINT

LOCATION:    51° 20′ 20″ N. 01° 29′ 30″ E.

The Greypoint was torpedoed by a German torpedo boat destroyer and sank on 8th March 1917. The location given was 'SE by E from Broadstairs'. Not exactly precise, but a start.

## 94. Unknown

LOCATION:    52° 00′ 10″ N. 01° 49′ 10″ E.

A fairly large wreck first located in 1971. The survey report stated that there was at least 28 metres (92 feet) of water over the wreck, but did not give the general depths. The echo sounder readings indicated that it was a cargo-type vessel.

The area is not noted for underwater visibility, although after a period of settled weather it can be as much as 15 feet. An interesting point—the tidal range around here is only 2 feet.

## 95. Unknown

LOCATION:    52° 00′ 25″ N. 01° 35′ 46″ E.

This wreck, located in 1964, is reported as being 'a comparatively small wreck—possibly a submarine'. It stands about 7 feet high in general depths of 45 feet—a good club boat dive. The position has since been confirmed.

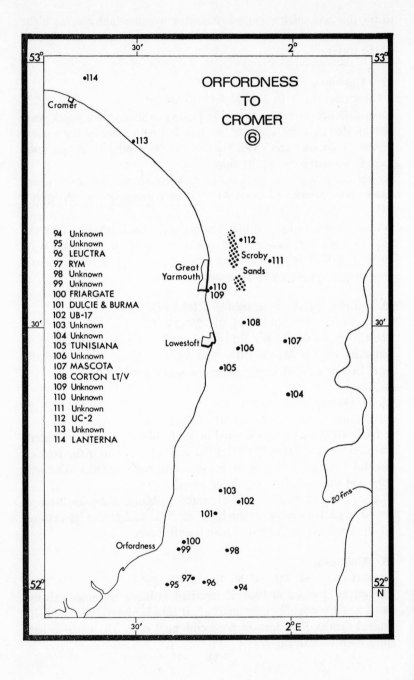

ORFORDNESS
TO
CROMER
⑥

94 Unknown
95 Unknown
96 LEUCTRA
97 RYM
98 Unknown
99 Unknown
100 FRIARGATE
101 DULCIE & BURMA
102 UB-17
103 Unknown
104 Unknown
105 TUNISIANA
106 Unknown
107 MASCOTA
108 CORTON LT/V
109 Unknown
110 Unknown
111 Unknown
112 UC-2
113 Unknown
114 LANTERNA

•114
Cromer
•113

•112
Scroby •111
Sands
Great
Yarmouth
•110
109

•108
Lowestoft
•106 •107
•105
•104

•103
•102
101•

Orfordness
•100
•99 •98
•95 97• •96 •94

20 fms

Horizontal sextant fixes are: Felixstowe Church Spire 12° 28′ to small lattice mast, 84° 03′ to Orfordness Lighthouse.

### 96. British merchant steamship LEUCTRA
LOCATION: 52° 00′ 48″ N. 01° 43′ 24″ E.

A vessel of 3027 tons gross, the Leuctra was torpedoed and sunk on 12th January 1915, '1½ miles SE by S from the Shipwash Lighthouse'. With such a large tonnage, this should be quite a substantial wreck—if you can find it.

### 97. Norwegian merchant steamship RYM
LOCATION: 52° 01′ 14″ N. 01° 41′ 10″ E.

The Rym was a vessel of 1073 tons gross, 624 tons net, with dimensions of 228·2 × 35·1 × 14·5. She was built, of steel and with one deck, in 1908 by Fredstadmek Vaerks, and was owned at the time of loss by J. Lund and Co. The sinking occurred on 14th July 1915, and was caused by a torpedo from a German submarine. The cargo was coal.

This wreck was originally buoyed for many years. Unfortunately, the buoy line snapped during a heavy storm, and the wreck has never been re-located. It is recorded that just before the buoy was lost, there was 20 feet of water over the wreck at low water springs.

### 98. Unknown
LOCATION: 52° 04′ 21″ N. 01° 47′ 56″ E.

This wreck was first located in 1931, and would appear to be a large one. There is at least 60 feet of water over the wreck at low water springs, and the surrounding area averages 80 feet. So the wreck itself stands some 20 feet high on the sea bed.

Although underwater visibility is limited in this area, Wreck 98 is some distance from the coast, where visibility is somewhat better.

Bearing and distance from the Orfordness Lighthouse is: 94° 20′, 8·27 miles.

### 99. Unknown
LOCATION: 52° 04′ 32″ N. 01° 38′ 01″ E.

This wreck was first located in 1964, and the position has since been confirmed. The least amount of water over the remains at low water springs is 32 feet, in surrounding depths of 45 feet, so the wreck stands some 13 feet high.

This position is in the approximate area of the sinking of the Friargate (Wreck 100)—could this be it? It seems unlikely, because the Friargate sank some 39 years before this wreck was located. In which case, what is the name of this wreck? And where is the Friargate?

Horizontal sextant fixes are: Bawdsey South Tall Radar Mast 43° 35′ to Orford Light, 58° 53′ to the wreck mast. Or, bearing and distance from Orfordness Lighthouse: 102½° 2·18 miles.

### 100. British merchant steamship FRIARGATE
LOCATION:   52° 05′ 20″ N. 01° 39′ 15″ E.

The Friargate was a fairly small vessel of 264 tons gross, 97 tons net. Built of steel, with one deck, in 1910, by Crabtree and Co., of Yarmouth, the owners at the time of loss were A. Chester of Middlesborough.

While carrying a cargo of loam on 3rd November 1915, the Friargate struck a mine and sank with the loss of 2 lives.

As mentioned, there is an unknown wreck (99) in the vicinity, and it is not impossible—although highly unlikely— that this is the Friargate. Perhaps the next time a subaqua club is diving the area....

### 101. British steamships DULCIE and BURMA
LOCATION:   52° 08′ 30″ N. 01° 45′ 15″ E.

Two for the price of one. It is worth mentioning that early records show that dispersal operations were at one time scheduled for the Burma. But Trinity House has never recorded either wreck as 'position confirmed', so there is some doubt. However, it is possible that the location of at least one of these wrecks is residing in an old and dusty file somewhere.

The first vessel is the Dulcie. This one was of 2033 tons gross, 1095 tons net, and had dimensions of 275 × 41·6 × 17·8. She was built of steel, in 1900, by W. Gray and Co. Ltd, of West Hartlepool. The owner at the time of loss was C. Nielson of West Hartlepool.

The Dulcie was torpedoed and sank on 19th June 1915, while carrying a cargo of coal.

The second vessel is the Burma, a smaller vessel of 706 tons gross with dimensions of 203·3 × 30·1 × 13·5. This was built of steel, in 1891, by S. P. Austin and Sons, and the owner at the time of loss was the Bennett Steamship Company.

The Burma struck a mine and sank on 23rd June 1916.

## 102. German submarine UB-17
LOCATION: 52° 10′ 00″ N. 01° 50′ 00″ E.

This submarine had a surface displacement of 127 tons, and an underwater displacement of 142 tons, with dimensions of 91·2 × 9·75 (beam).

The UB-17 was originally sighted or located by HMS Onslow. During the chase, Onslow dropped depth charges and sank the UB-17 on 11th March 1918.

I have heard tales—no more than that—that divers have visited a wrecked submarine in this area. But to the best of my knowledge the UB-17 has never been located.

## 103. Unknown
LOCATION: 52° 11′ 28″ N. 01° 46′ 10″ E.

This is a large wreck which was first located in 1931, and several surveys have since confirmed the position.

There is about 79 feet of water over the wreck at low water springs, and the surrounding area is 100 feet deep, so the remains stand over 21 feet high.

As mentioned, the wreck is quite substantial and the remains cover quite a large area, so much so that there is a considerable and noticeable swirl on the surface when the tide is running—a point well worth bearing in mind.

Horizontal sextant fixes are also available: Orfordness Lighthouse 35° 36′ to Thorp East Water Tower, 66° 44′ to Walberswick Church Tower.

## 104. Unknown
LOCATION: 52° 22′ 07″ N. 01° 59′ 28″ E.

This could be one of the largest 'unknown' wrecks on the list. It was originally thought to be the remains of a steamer called the Frumenton, but the wreck of this vessel has been found elsewhere —so what is this?

First located in 1942, the position has been confirmed. The wreck stands an impressive 40 feet high on a sea bed 82 feet deep.

It has been dived by a subaqua club, who reported 'a vessel of at least 1000 tons; the centre of the wreck has suffered an explosion— possibly a mine or torpedo. There is wreckage all over the bed.'

There are several points here. It is unlikely that a vessel of only 1000 tons would stand 40 feet high, unless there is some object like a mast sticking up. Could this be a typing error that should have read 10,000 tons? And the fact that there is wreckage all over the place, at that depth, could indicate that salvage or dispersal operations have taken place. In any case, it seems strange that such a vessel should have been visited and yet the name is still unknown. But this only serves to highlight the problem of the unknown wrecks.

Horizontal sextant fixes are: Southwold Church Tower 43° 42′ to St Luke's Cupola at Lowestoft, 15° 01′ to Hapton High Mast.

### 105. British merchant steamship TUNISIANA
LOCATION: 52° 25′ 37″ N. 01° 46′ 11″ E.

This is another big one—if you can find it. The Tunisiana was a vessel of 4220 tons gross, 2757 tons net, with dimensions of 360·2 × 48 × 20·2. Built in 1906, of steel and with one deck, by the Northumberland Steamship Company of Newcastle, the owners at the time of loss were Furness Whitby and Company of London. The Tunisiana was torpedoed and sunk on 23rd June 1915 while carrying a cargo of wheat.

For a while after the time of loss two masts were distinctly visible above water at low tide. It is probably because of this that no accurate fix was ever taken. Anyway, after a while—probably after a storm—these masts vanished. The site is not very far from Lowestoft and must be worth a visit.

### 106. Unknown
LOCATION: 52° 27′ 46″ N. 01° 59′ 28″ E.

This looks like a fairly large wreck. It was first located in 1951, and the survey vessel reported a 'very good echo contact'. It stands some 23 feet high in a depth of 83 feet, and is over 200 feet in length. There is a small 3-foot scour at the side, and it is lying 040° by 220°.

This is also not far out from Lowestoft and must be worth a visit after a spell of calm weather to settle the visibility.

Horizontal sextant fixes are: Kingsland Church Tower 33° 58′ to Kirkley Church Tower, 47° 08′ to Corton Church Tower.

### 107. Armed British merchant steamship MASCOTA
LOCATION: 52° 28′ 30″ N. 01° 58′ 30″ E.

A 674 tons gross vessel, the Mascota was captured by a German torpedo boat destroyer (TBD). Seven of the crew were made prisoners, then the TBD sank the Mascota. This was on the 23rd March 1917.

The area of sinking has general depths of 84 feet.

No accurate fix was taken—although possibly the Germans took one. However, the keen wreck detective will note with interest that 7 of the crew (was this all of them?) were captured. If any of them are still alive, perhaps they could give some more definite fix.

### 108. Light vessel CORTON

LOCATION: 52° 30′ 30″ N. 01° 50′ 30″ E.

The light vessel Corton struck a mine and sank on 21st June 1916. Five lives were lost. Reports of that time stated that the vessel literally went down in minutes, so the wreck should not be too far from the site of the explosion.

The area of sinking is between Lowestoft and the 20 fathom line, in general depths of 120 feet. The position given above is the fix of the original station, so this would be the starting point for a search.

### 109. Unknown

LOCATION: 52° 34′ 25″ N. 01° 44′ 09″ E.

This wreck lies close inshore, at the southern end of Great Yarmouth.

The Hydrographic Department records state: 'In 1971 a vessel was stranded in this position, lying NE by SW on Spending Beach. An attempt was to have been made to remove the wreck, but legal difficulties made this impossible'. Apparently, the wreck then slid back into deeper water.

I must confess that this one is a puzzle which I have meant to investigate for some time. If the date—1971—is accurate, surely the authorities knew the name of the vessel. Or is it an error, and the date should read 1917 or something? It seems rather odd, but there it is. Perhaps some local divers could shed some light on the problem.

### 110. Unknown

LOCATION: 52° 34′ 45″ N. 01° 44′ 39″ E.

This is very near the previous wreck, slightly farther out. It lies in 18 feet of water at low water springs.

The vessel is reputed to have beached around 1930, broken in two, then slipped back into deeper water. Many divers have visited the wreck—there are at least six 'dive reports' on file—but there is still no indication as to the name of the vessel.

Horizontal sextant fixes are: Hockton High Mast 90° 03′ to Caulston Church, 71° 57′ to Nelson's Monument.

### 111. Unknown
LOCATION: 52° 37′ 38″ N. 01° 55′ 39″ E.

Very little is known about this wreck, which lies out from Great Yarmouth, on the seaward side of the Scroby Sands. There is, however, a mass of technical or mathematical data.

First located in 1951, the wreck stands 21 feet high in general depths of 114 feet. It is approximately 250 feet in length and is lying 170° by 350°.

This must be a substantial wreck. It stands high, and judging by its length is certainly not 'on end'.

### 112. German submarine UC-2
LOCATION: 52° 40′ 00″ N. 01° 50′ 00″ E.

The submarine UC-2 had a displacement of 168–182 tons, with dimensions of 111·5 × 10·5 (beam).

It sank after being rammed by the steamer Cottingham, on the north-east side of the Scroby Sands on 2nd July 1915.

To the best of my knowledge, the UC-2 has never been located. Perhaps if you could locate any of the crew of the Cottingham, a more accurate fix might be obtained.

### 113. Unknown
LOCATION: 52° 51′ 08″ N. 01° 29′ 12″ E.

This one was first reported by Trinity House in 1948, in a statement that said 'This wreck is a menace to small inshore craft'. It is a shallow one—in fact it dries a couple of feet at low water springs, so this is the time to locate it.

### 114. British merchant steamship LANTERNA
LOCATION: 52° 58′ 27″ N. 01° 19′ 10″ E.

In this general position the 1685 tons gross vessel Lanterna struck

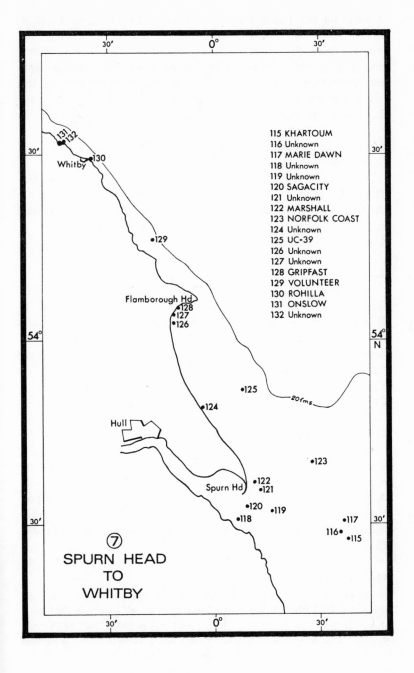

115 KHARTOUM
116 Unknown
117 MARIE DAWN
118 Unknown
119 Unknown
120 SAGACITY
121 Unknown
122 MARSHALL
123 NORFOLK COAST
124 Unknown
125 UC-39
126 Unknown
127 Unknown
128 GRIPFAST
129 VOLUNTEER
130 ROHILLA
131 ONSLOW
132 Unknown

Whitby

Flamborough Hd

Hull

Spurn Hd

20 fms

⑦
SPURN HEAD
TO
WHITBY

N

a mine on 6th October 1916, 2½ miles NE ½ E. from Cromer'. It is worth noting that the Lanterna did not sink immediately, and was last seen sinking slowly. No one actually saw her go down, and it is possible that she drifted quite far overnight before sinking. If this is the case, and bearing in mind the tidal flows in this area, it is within the realms of possibility that Wreck 113 is the Lanterna.

### 115. British merchant steamship KHARTOUM
LOCATION: 53° 27' 12" N. 00° 38' 18" E.
This vessel, of 3020 tons gross, struck a mine and sank on 27th November 1914.
As usual in such cases, nobody bothered to take a fix—and who can blame them! General sea bed depths are 50 feet.
Could this be Wreck 116?

### 116. Unknown
LOCATION: 53° 28' 30" N. 00° 36' 09" E.
This wreck is presumed to have sunk around 1916, because in February 1916 a wreck was reported in this position 'with masts showing at low water'. However, the masts soon vanished in heavy seas, and a 1918 survey confirmed the position giving a 'least depth over the wreck' of 54 feet.
This is the area in which the Khartoum sank in 1914.
Could this be the site of the wreck?

### 117. British merchant steamship MARIE DAWN
LOCATION: 53° 30' 24" N. 00° 37' 12" E.
The Marie Dawn, a vessel of 2157 tons gross, was bombed by enemy aircraft and sank on 3rd November 1941.
A 1942 survey reported 'wreck located in this position'. But in 1962 another survey could not locate it here. In 1972, yet another survey visited the area and reported 'obstruction at 00° 37' 10"'.
Could *this* be the Marie Dawn?

### 118. Unknown
LOCATION: 53° 30' 45" N. 00° 06' 36" E.
I have very little information about this wreck—except that it is there. It was first located in 1946, and the position has been confirmed. The only other information I have is that it dries at low

water springs. Someone in the area must have dived on it. Does anyone know the name?

## 119. Unknown

LOCATION: 53° 32′ 07″ N. 00° 16′ 23″ E.

On the 15th February 1940, the vessel Castor reported that she had struck a wreck in this position. A subsequent survey confirmed the location and stated that the wreck was about 18 feet high, in general depths of 40 feet. According to this information the wreck should be quite substantial and well worth a visit.

Horizontal sextant fixes are: Donna Noak Flagstaff 66° 35′ to Spurn Head Lighthouse, 22° 28′ to Kilnsea South Tower.

## 120. Steamer SAGACITY

LOCATION: 53° 33′ 05″ N. 00° 08′ 54″ E.

This vessel, of 490 tons gross, sank on 28th October 1940, '148° 4,000 yards from Spurn Main Light'.

That is all I have on my records, but such a recent wreck should not be short of documentation. This, and the proximity to shore, should make it a good subject for the wreck detective.

## 121. Unknown

LOCATION: 53° 35′ 30″ N. 00° 13′ 14″ E.

This wreck was first located during a 1959 survey, and successive surveys have confirmed the position.

It lies on a bed of sand and shells, standing about 14 feet high in general depths of 45 feet. There is a deep scour at one side, indicative of fairly strong currents—a point to bear in mind for diving clubs who might think that the relatively shallow depths would suit beginners.

Could this be the wreck of the Sagacity? It was certainly located after she was sunk, and lies near the area of sinking. The strong currents could certainly have carried the Sagacity this far if she did not sink too quickly.

Horizontal sextant fixes are: Spurn Lighthouse 45° 09′ to South Kilnsea Tower, 01° 04′ to North Kilnsea Tower. The latter, you might note, is a very narrow angle.

## 122. British merchant steamship MARSHALL

LOCATION: 53° 37′ 00″ N. 00° 11′ 00″ E.

The Marshall was of 307 tons gross, and was built in Shields in

1846. The owner at the time of loss was the Elbe and Humber Steamship Company.

While on route from Hamburg to Hull, with 30 passengers and crew, the Marshall collided with the barque Woodhouse, *twice*, on 26th November 1853, '5 miles from the Newsand Float of Kilnsea', and was never seen again—afloat, that is.

Shortly after the collision, one of the Marshall's boats was found floating, and near this, North Sea fishermen reported seeing the tops of the masts at low tide. These, along with the fix, have vanished.

### 123. British merchant steamship NORFOLK COAST
LOCATION :   53° 40' 00" N. 00° 28' 00" E.

A vessel of 782 tons gross, 382 tons net, and with dimensions of 195 × 30 × 11·6, the Norfolk Coast was built of steel, with one deck, by W. Harkess and Sons of Middlesborough, in 1910.

She sank on 18th June 1918, after being torpedoed by a German submarine. 8 lives were lost. However, the captain survived, and some records might be available if someone is prepared to do some research. The owner at the time of loss was Coast Lines of London.

The position given above is the generally accepted one, but one other report at the time gave the position as 53° *56'* 00" N.

### 124. Unknown
LOCATION :   53° 49' 96" N. 00° 03' 36" W.

This one is so close inshore that the top dries at low water springs. The Hydrographic Department records show that this wreck was first located or reported in 1964. This is surprising considering that the top dries and is visible. Has the shifting sea bed 'lifted' the wreck to shallow water? What is the answer?

### 125. German submarine UC-39
LOCATION :   53° 52' 00" N. 00° 08' 00" E.

The UC-39 had a surface displacement of 400 tons, and an underwater displacement of 511 tons, with dimensions of 162–170 × 17 (beam).

A destroyer, HMS Thrasher, sighted the UC-39 on 8th February 1917, depth charged the area and sank the submarine. The above location is the one given at the time of loss, although successive surveys have failed to locate the wreck.

### 126. Unknown
LOCATION:  54° 02′ 51″ N. 00° 11′ 51″ W.
This wreck is close inshore in shallow water. It was first reported to the authorities in 1965, and is marked on subsequent Admiralty Charts as 'an obstruction on the sea bed'. What sort of obstruction?

### 127. Unknown
LOCATION:  54° 04′ 13″ N. 00° 11′ 26″ W.
Another one lying close inshore. This wreck was first located by a subaqua diver in 1971, and the position has been confirmed. The diver's report only states that 'the wreck is 10 feet high'. Trinity House sent a vessel to investigate the site, and found that there was 10 feet of water over the wreck—making a general depth of 20 feet. The Trinity House survey also scheduled the wreck for dispersal. Fine, but what was it?

### 128. British steamship GRIPFAST
LOCATION:  54° 05′ 00″ N. 00° 10′ 30″ W.
A vessel of 1109 tons gross with dimensions of 225 × 35 × 13, the Gripfast was on route from Barry to Sheerness when she was sunk by gunfire from an enemy vessel on 29th January 1940.
This is another wreck lying close inshore, just south of Flamborough Head. The site should be well worth a visit—if someone hasn't already done so.

### 129. British iron steamship VOLUNTEER
LOCATION:  54° 16′ 20″ N. 00° 17′ 15″ W.
This was a vessel of 607 tons gross, with dimensions of 208 × 25·2 × 13·7, built in 1861.
While on route from Leith to Rotterdam with a general cargo, the Volunteer ran ashore on the 'rocks 3 miles north of Filey Brig', and promptly sank. This was on the 18th February 1865.
The site of loss lies just short of the 20 fathom line. If the Volunteer in fact crossed this line before she sank, then this is not a search job for amateur divers. If not, the Volunteer should be in about 80 feet of water.

### 130. British liner ROHILLA
LOCATION: 54° 29′ 21″ N. 00° 35′ 42″ W.

Owned by the India Steam Navigation Company, the Rohilla was of 7891 tons gross, with dimensions of 460 × 56 × 30·6, and was built in 1906 at Harland and Wolff.

Converted to a hospital ship during World War One, the Rohilla was on route from Leith to Dunkirk to bring wounded soldiers back from France when she ran on rocks, at night, a half mile south of Whitby in a violent ESE gale. Tremendous seas were running. In the morning, three bodies plus some wreckage were washed ashore north of Whitby. At first the Whitby lifeboat could not even get out to sea, but later made two visits to the stricken ship, bringing back 34 survivors in all.

Rockets were fired at the wreck. One of them made it and a line was secured, but it snapped before it could be used.

Shortly after, the Rohilla broke in two and slipped into the sea on 30th October 1914. There were 229 people on board, and 83 of them were lost.

There must be something remaining of such a large vessel, and the site must be worth a visit.

### 131. British cargo steamship ONSLOW
LOCATION: 54° 32′ 10″ N. 00° 43′ 30″ W.

The Onslow was a vessel of 2722 tons gross, with dimensions of 312 × 45·9 × 20·5, and was built in 1890. The owners at the time of loss were Scaramanga Brothers.

While on route from Sunderland to Piraeus with a cargo of coal, the Onslow was wrecked 'at Kettleness Point near Whitby' on 12th August 1911.

Like the Rohilla, the Onslow was a large vessel, lies close inshore, and must be worth a visit.

### 132. Unknown
LOCATION: 54° 32′ 30″ N. 00° 42′ 20″ W.

This wreck was first reported in 1918, when the upper works were showing at low water springs. These vanished below the surface in 1919. Nothing more has ever been reported, and no attempt at identification has ever been made. Perhaps some local club could dive the site and send in a report.

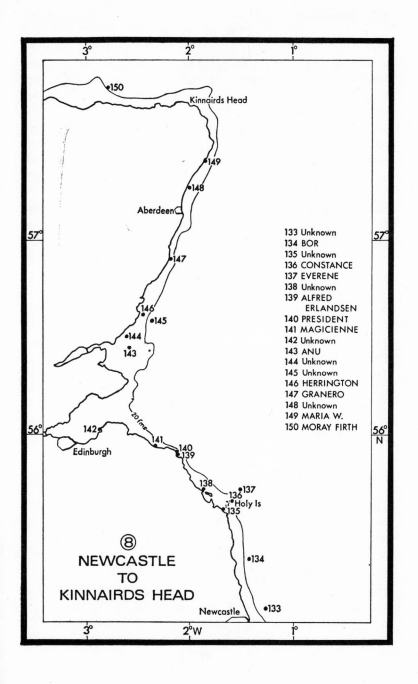

133 Unknown
134 BOR
135 Unknown
136 CONSTANCE
137 EVERENE
138 Unknown
139 ALFRED
    ERLANDSEN
140 PRESIDENT
141 MAGICIENNE
142 Unknown
143 ANU
144 Unknown
145 Unknown
146 HERRINGTON
147 GRANERO
148 Unknown
149 MARIA W.
150 MORAY FIRTH

⑧
NEWCASTLE
TO
KINNAIRDS HEAD

### 133. Unknown

LOCATION:   55° 04′ 12″ N. 01° 16′ 03″ W.

This wreck lies 'over the edge' of the 20 fathom line. It was first located in 1968, and it is recorded that the depth to the top of the wreck is at least 142 feet, with surrounding depths of 171 feet. So a dive even to the top of the wreck is too deep for any but the very experienced diver.

The wreck is on a bed of shell and gravel, and there is a small scour at the side. It lies NE by SW, and is over 200 feet in length. This eliminates the possibility that it is standing 'on end', and means that the remains stand some 30 feet high—a large wreck indeed.

Horizontal sextant fixes are: Tynemouth North Breakwater Lighthouse 36° 38′ to St Mary's Lighthouse, 25° 30′ to the 'easternmost power station chimney of the four'.


### 134. Norwegian steamer BOR

LOCATION:   55° 20′ 00″ N. 01° 26′ 00″ W.

A vessel of 1149 tons gross, with dimensions of 228·9 × 36·2 × 15·8, the Bor was built in 1914 by Nylands Vaerksted of Norway. The Bor was torpedoed by a German submarine on 21st February 1918, and reportedly 'sank in 45 minutes'.

The location should be quite accurate because it was given by HMS Arab, which was in the area at the time and confirmed both the loss and position.

A word of warning. The wreck also lies over the 20 fathom line, so is probably in depths in excess of 150 feet.


### 135. Unknown

LOCATION:   55° 36′ 05″ N. 01° 40′ 51″ W.

This is a large wreck lying close inshore—in fact, it dries at low water springs. In such a position it is certain that many divers have visited the remains, yet there is nothing on the records to indicate the name. Can anyone help?


### 136. British motor fishing vessel CONSTANCE

LOCATION:   55° 38′ 36″ N. 01° 36′ 30″ W.

A small vessel—only 23 tons gross and 52 feet in length—the Constance went aground on the Farne Islands, '¼ east of Longstone

Lighthouse' on the 11th September 1972. Nothing else is known. If anyone wants a 'new' wreck . . .

### 137. Latvian merchant steamship EVERENE
LOCATION: 55° 42′ 15″ N. 01° 30′ 30″ W.

A fairly substantial vessel of 4434 tons gross, the Everene was built in 1906. The owners at the time of loss were Grauds.

On 25th January 1914, the Everene was torpedoed and sank. It would appear that she did not sink immediately, because various positions are given for the location. This indicates that the vessel floated a while before sinking—although I could be wrong here. Some of the alternatives to the position given above are: 'South of the Farne Islands' and '4–5 miles east by south of the Longstone'.

### 138. Unknown
LOCATION: 55° 42′ 06″ N. 01° 52′ 16″ W.

I have very little information about this wreck, except that it was first located in 1934. At that time the top dried at low water springs, but I do not know if this still applies.

### 139. Danish steamship ALFRED ERLANDSEN
LOCATION: 55° 53′ 50″ N. 02° 07′ 30″ W.

A vessel of 954 tons gross, with dimensions of 207·6 × 31·2 × 14·1, the Alfred Erlandsen was built in 1890.

On route to Grangemouth, she was wrecked 'On Ebb Carrs Rock at Castle Point, St Abbs Head' on the 17th October 1907.

The first news about the wreck was received at Dunbar, with the information that 'a steamer has stranded on the rocks below the village'. The Skateraw lifeboat was launched in the middle of the northerly gale that prevailed. Eyemouth Rocket Brigade and lifeboat were also summoned. At this time the Alfred Erlandsen was about 700 yards offshore. Rockets were fired, but they all fell short. The Eyemouth lifeboat could not reach the stricken vessel in the dark, but could hear cries for help from the crew. The lifeboat scoured the surrounding area for an hour, with torches, to see if they could pick up anyone who had been washed overboard, but without luck.

In the morning, at first light, only wreckage could be seen.

The site is close inshore, and possibly subaqua clubs have already dived the wreck. If this is so, the Hydrographic Department would like to hear from them.

## 140. British steamer PRESIDENT
LOCATION:    55° 54′ 00″ N. 02° 07′ 30″ W.

This particular area is studded with wrecks, and one of them is the 1945 tons gross President. She was built in 1907, with dimensions of 280 × 40·5 × 18·2, and was on route from Hamburg to Methill, in ballast, when she came ashore at Whapness near Eyemouth on the 29th April 1928. She then slid back into deeper water and was never seen again. Or was she?

In 1967 a group of RAF divers reported locating a wreck 'one quarter of a mile SE of St Abbs Head', in the above position. Is this the President? The RAF divers found no evidence to substantiate a name. Perhaps some local divers can.

## 141. Danish auxiliary wooden schooner MAGICIENNE
LOCATION:    55° 56′ 00″ N. 02° 19′ 45″ W.

This would be a rather interesting, different wreck to locate. The Magicienne, a vessel of 248 tons gross, with dimensions of 116·3 × 27·2 × 18·8, was built in 1912.

On route from the Faeroes to Blyth with a cargo of salt, the Magicienne went ashore on the 3rd May 1940. Later, she slipped off into deeper water.

## 142. Unknown
LOCATION:    56° 01′ 21″ N. 02° 52′ 45″ W.

All I know about this wreck is that it lies close inshore, was first located in 1969, and dries at low water springs. Does anyone know more?

## 143. Estonian coaster ANU
LOCATION:    56° 26′ 54″ N. 02° 35′ 41″ W.

This is really an unknown wreck first located by a survey ship in 1969. The report states that the wreck 'is scattered over 200 feet, on a bed of sand, and stands only 5 feet high in general depths of 70 feet. It is lying 145° by 225° and there is a 6-foot scour at the side.'

It just happens that the location given by the survey ship is identical to that given by the Anu when she sank on 6th July 1940—

a relatively recent wreck. Could this be her resting place?
The Anu was of 1421 tons gross, with dimensions of 250 × 36·2 × 17·6, and was built in 1883.
Is this the wreck of the Anu? If not, where is she, and what is the wreck the survey located?

## 144. Unknown
LOCATION: 56° 30′ 16″ N. 02° 36′ 30″ W.
This wreck was first located in 1969. It is about 300 feet in length, lying NE by SW, and stands about 15 feet high in general depths of 70 feet. There is a fairly deep scour of 10 feet at the side, which indicates that there are strong currents at certain periods of the tide.
The length and height suggest a large wreck that could prove well worth a visit.

## 145. Unknown
LOCATION: 56° 35′ 20″ N. 02° 21′ 30″ W.
This is a very large wreck which was first located when the trawler Camelia fouled its anchor at this site on the 15th September 1930. Latest surveys indicate that the wreck is about 25 feet high, 280 feet in length, and lying NNW by SSE.
I have included this one mainly for the armchair wreck detective. Its size might make it easier to research because all smaller vessels can be eliminated. And the reason why I stipulate *armchair* detective is because the depth—about 205 feet—is much too deep for the amateur diver.

## 146. British merchant steamship HERRINGTON
LOCATION: 56° 37′ 00″ N. 02° 27′ 00″ W.
The Herrington was a vessel of 1258 tons gross, and was mined and sunk on the 4th May 1917 '¾ mile ESE from Red Head at Forfar'.
And that is all. Nothing else has ever been reported about the Herrington. But it was a vessel of decent size and as such is well worth looking for.

## 147. Norwegian steamship GRANERO
LOCATION: 56° 54′ 28″ N. 02° 11′ 18″ W.
This vessel was of 1318 tons gross, and was built in 1913.

While on route to Alloa with a cargo of pit props, the Granero went ashore 'on the south side of Crawton Ness, 4 miles south of Stonehaven, on the 23rd October 1933'.

There is some inconsistency here. The records of the Receiver of Wrecks at Aberdeen contain a reference that reads 'A firm brought ashore some scrap reputed to be from the Granero. They found it 1 mile due east of Crawton Ness in 45 feet of water'. This is a different position to the one given, which has general depths much deeper than 45 feet. It might be worth a visit to Aberdeen, to see whether the scrap was eventually identified as that of the Granero. If not, where did the scrap come from?

### 148. Unknown
LOCATION: 57° 24′ 00″ N. 02° 00′ 00″ W.

This wreck was first located in 1952, when the trawler Kathleen lost a trawl. Another trawler recovered the trawl and stated that there was a wreck in 25 feet of water.

Later, divers visited the wreck and said that it was 'a large steel vessel'. Unfortunately, they could not get more information because the visibility was only 2–3 feet. It sounds unlikely that those divers, or others, have never visited the site again. If they have, perhaps they have more definite information as to the name of the vessel.

### 149. Dutch motor vessel MARIA W
LOCATION: 57° 24′ 00″ N. 01° 51′ 00″ W.

This vessel was registered in Rotterdam and was on route from Ghent to Scrabster with a cargo of fertilizer when she went aground on the 22nd February 1966.

A report at that time stated that 'the bridge is above water level, the vessel lying in a rocky gulley'. But no accurate position was given and the bridge soon vanished from sight in the heavy seas.

### 150. British merchant steamship MORAY FIRTH
LOCATION: 57° 46′ 00″ N. 02° 47′ 00″ W.

All that is known is that the Moray Firth, a vessel of 541 tons gross, sank after a collision (who with?) on the 28th March 1943. This is not too far back in time, and there should be plenty of local documentation in local papers, etc., to do some research.

3. H.M.S. Foyle, which was sunk by a mine on 15 March 1917. Is this Wreck 23, which was discovered by Kingston Subaqua Club? (*Imperial War Museum*)

4. H.M.S. Viper, wrecked in thick fog on 3 August 1901. If this is Wreck 274, it would be of particular interest to historians. (*Imperial War Museum*)

5. Another photograph of H.M.S. Viper. (*Imperial War Museum*)

6. This is the concrete collier that was sunk to be used as a wharf during World War II. Does anyone know the name? (*Imperial War Museum*)

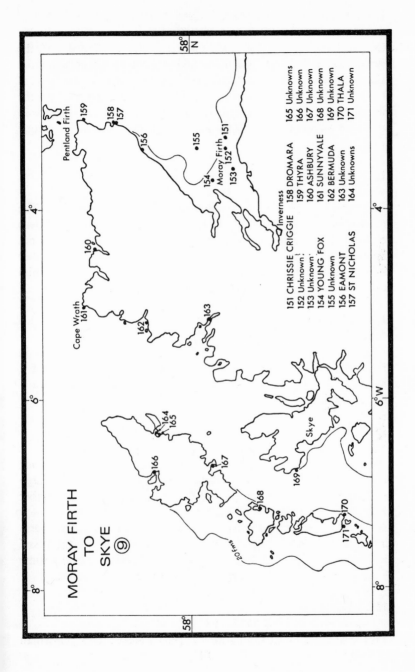

MORAY FIRTH
TO
SKYE
⑨

Pentland Firth

Cape Wrath

Inverness

Moray Firth

Skye

20 fms.

151 CHRISSIE CRIGGIE
152 Unknown
153 Unknown
154 YOUNG FOX
155 Unknown
156 EAMONT
157 ST NICHOLAS

158 DROMARA
159 THYRA
160 ASHBURY
161 SUNNYVALE
162 BERMUDA
163 Unknown
164 Unknowns

165 Unknowns
166 Unknown
167 Unknown
168 Unknown
169 Unknown
170 THALA
171 Unknown

### 151. British merchant fishing vessel CHRISSIE CRIGGIE
LOCATION: 57° 47′ 00″ N. 03° 14′ 00″ W.

On the 1st December 1971, the Chrissie Criggie collided with the motor fishing vessel Spectrum and sank 4 miles NNE from Lossiemouth.

No accurate fix was taken at the time, and it is likely that the wreck will remain undiscovered because the general depths in this area—averaging 150 feet—are too deep to warrant a subaqua survey.

### 152. Unknown
LOCATION: 57° 47′ 09″ N. 03° 20′ 00″ W.

This wreck is reputed to be that of a Wellington bomber. The records of the Hydrographic Department state that the wreck was reported in 1963 by a 'Lt Com Ralph'—and that's all. I do not know who the gentleman is, and the records carry no further information. But it should not be too difficult to locate him through Navy records, and get the whole story.

### 153. Unknown
LOCATION: 57° 44′ 49″ N. 03° 33′ 56″ W.

As with Wreck 152, this was first reported by Lt Com Ralph in 1963. Apparently he considered that the remains are those of a 'wooden vessel'. I do not know how he came by this information, but it might be worth following up.

### 154. British auxiliary motor sailing vessel YOUNG FOX
LOCATION: 57° 52′ 00″ N. 03° 41′ 00″ W.

A relatively small vessel of 98 tons gross, built in 1893, the Young Fox was on route from Sunderland to Portmalomack with a cargo of 139½ tons of coal when she 'went missing' on the 6th December 1928, 'about 3 miles east of Tarbat Ness'.

Apparently the weather was very rough on this date. The storm lasted the whole day, so it is impossible to guess where the vessel went down unless the hour of sinking is known. Perhaps some local papers have this information—or some other details.

### 155. Unknown
LOCATION: 57° 57′ 55″ N. 03° 29′ 44″ W.

This is another of Lt Com Ralph's '1963 wrecks'. This gentleman certainly seems to have been a keen wreck detective. Apparently he went through local records after making sure that the obstruction he had found was definitely a wreck, and came to the conclusion that it was the remains of a ferry. Can anyone add anything else?

### 156. British steam trawler EAMONT
LOCATION: 58° 16′ 30″ N. 03° 22′ 00″ W.
This trawler of 227 tons gross, 87 tons net, and built in 1916, had dimensions of 117·4 × 22·5 × 13·7.
She was bombed by German aircraft on 11th February 1941. A bomb fell directly into the wheelhouse, but failed to explode. The vessel was abandoned immediately, and was last seen drifting ashore '3 cables north of Latheron Wheel Harbour'.
Of course, no accurate fix was taken at the time. There is a report, unconfirmed because the source is not known, that the wreck was located and the bomb removed. However it must be stressed that this report is unconfirmed—so if you find the wreck do not enter it but report the location to the nearest authority.

### 157. British steamer ST NICHOLAS
LOCATION: 58° 26′ 15″ N. 03° 03′ 30″ W.
This iron hulled steamer was of 787 tons gross, 445 tons net, was built in 1877 and had dimensions of 227·5 × 27·2 × 15·4.
While on route from Scrabster to Wick, with a general cargo, she ran ashore on Proudfoot Rocks on 17th June 1914. The following day she slid off the rocks into 70 feet of water.
If the St Nicholas floated a while before she sank, then the wreck might be difficult to locate. But if she was badly holed and full of water, she might be lying close to the rocks—therefore an easy visit.

### 158. British steamer DROMARA
LOCATION: 58° 26′ 30″ N. 03° 03′ 30″ W.
The Dromara was of 723 tons gross, 291 tons net, was built in 1921 and had dimensions of 181 × 30·7 × 13·5. She was equipped with triple expansion machinery.
While on route from Londonderry to London with a cargo of bog ore (is there such a material?) the cargo shifted and the steamer listed severely. The crew immediately abandoned the vessel and

she ran ashore on 14th February 1941, at the foot of the Old Man of Wick.

The site is very near that of the St Nicholas, so the area should be well worth exploring.

### 159. Steamer THYRA

LOCATION: 58° 36′ 30″ N. 03° 01′ 18″ W.

The Thyra was of 3742 tons gross, 2419 tons net, was built in 1899 and had dimensions of 339 × 48 × 29—a substantial vessel. While on route from Dundee to New York with a general cargo, she ran ashore at Duncansby Head on 11th June 1914. Some of the cargo was salvaged before she slipped back into the sea.

This position is near the northernmost point of the Scottish mainland, near the treacherous Pentland Firth. However, the site is close inshore, and to a certain extent protected from the currents, which tend to flow from the west. The size alone makes the wreck worth looking for.

### 160. Armed British merchant steamship ASHBURY

LOCATION: 58° 32′ 48″ N. 04° 24′ 32″ W.

This is a precise location, the only doubt being whether this is in fact the Ashbury.

This steamship was of 3901 tons gross, was built in 1924 by W. Gray & Co., and had dimensions of 356 × 50 × 24·7.

While on route from Workington to the Tyne, in ballast, the Ashbury foundered on 8th January 1945. All the crew—42 of them— were lost.

The position given above was reported by a Mr Muir in 1970, and he stated 'In 70 feet of water is the Ashbury'. Could someone confirm this?

The area, incidentally, is covered with wrecks, mostly named ones. This is because the Hydrographic Department has carried out very few surveys along this stretch of water. So there must be many unknown wrecks in addition, just waiting to be found.

### 161. British motor vessel SUNNYDALE

LOCATION: 58° 36′ 30″ N. 05° 01′ 00″ W.

On 16th December 1971, the Sunnydale 'came ashore 1 mile south of Cape Wrath'. I have no further information. Does anyone else have anything to add?

## 162. Passenger vessel BERMUDA
LOCATION:   58° 15′ 03″ N. 05° 11′ 30″ W.

The Bermuda was a very large vessel of 19,086 tons gross, 11,281 tons net, was built in 1927 and had dimensions of 525·9 × 74·1 × 45. She was driven by four screws.

On 19th November 1931, the Bermuda caught fire at Belfast and was severely damaged. The burnt hulk was purchased by Workman Clark Ltd, of Belfast, who sold it to Metal Industries Ltd. She left Belfast on 27th April 1933, in tow, for Rosyth, but parted tow and drifted ashore at Eddrachilles Bay on 30th April and became a total wreck.

A 1933 report stated that the wreck was 40 feet high on the sea bed, and the bearing and distance was: 187° 3·75 cables from Eilean Leah.

## 163. Unknown
LOCATION:   57° 53′ 45″ N. 05° 09′ 18″ W.

Ullapool is a fishing village and resort. Boats are available and the diving is fabulous. Situated on the eastern side of Loch Broom, which is open to the sea, the immediate waters are relatively sheltered. Plenty of wrecks lie around, including one near the jetty in 50 feet of water. It is a long time since I dived this area, but at that time the wreck mentioned was of name unknown. Has the situation changed? I would be surprised if it has not, but I don't know anyone who can tell me the name of the wreck.

## 164. Unknown (two wrecks)
LOCATIONS:   58° 12′ 12″ N. 06° 22′ 57″ W.
　　　　　　　58° 12′ 12″ N. 06° 22′ 52″ W.

These two wrecks, the names of which are unknown, lie so close together that they have been listed together—as has Wreck(s) 165. Both wrecks were first located in 1929, and the positions have been confirmed. They both lie inshore in shallow water, and both dry slightly at low water, so they should be easy to find.

## 165. Unknown (two wrecks)
LOCATIONS:   58° 11′ 16″ N. 06° 22′ 44″ W.
　　　　　　　58° 11′ 43″ N. 06° 22′ 32″ W.

As mentioned above, these wrecks lie so close together that they have been listed under the same number. They were first reported in 1958, and the positions have been confirmed.

All four wrecks (these and 164) lie in the approaches to Stornoway, on the Isle of Lewis, and should be easily accessible—providing you can get to Lewis! These wrecks also dry at low water, and it seems incredible that four wrecks can lie in such shallow water, so near one another, and yet the names of all of them are unknown. On the other hand, perhaps someone in the area does know.

### 166. Unknown
LOCATION: 58° 12' 45" N. 06° 47' 00" W.

This wreck was first located in 1929, and the position has been confirmed.

The site is in Loch Roag, which is open to the sea at the north-west end. Because this side receives wild Atlantic weather, I should not be surprised if the bottom of the Loch is not covered with wrecks.

### 167. Unknown
LOCATION: 57° 52' 34" N. 06° 41' 59" W.

Sheltered from the rough north-east weather, this is the site of a concrete collier which is used as a wharf. The remains are approximately 200 feet in length. It was sunk sometime during World War Two. It is a very large wreck which dries at low water. But nobody seems to know the name. Perhaps some of the locals remember the name of the vessel—but if so, this has not been recorded.

### 168. Unknown
LOCATION: 57° 35' 26" N. 07° 09' 03" W.

This wreck was first located in 1952, and dries at low water springs. The sea bed here is rocky.

I have never visited this area, but I understand that it is a good group of islands for a holiday, providing you don't demand a hectic night life.

### 169. Unknown
LOCATION: 57° 22' 10" N. 06° 42' 45" W.

This wreck, on the western side of the Isle of Skye, was first reported to Lloyds in October 1970.

The person who discovered the remains is a diver, a Mr Johnson, who stated in his report: 'On the Damsel Rocks are the remains of large iron hoops that appear to be part of a wreck. Some of the remains lie virtually on Damsel Rocks.'

If you ask the locals, they will tell you that a wreck did go down about here around 1935—but no one seems to know the name or any other particulars. Perhaps some local newspapers will hold some information.

It would be interesting to look at some of the pre-1930 local charts and maps. If these particular rocks had no name, or another name, prior to 1930, then it would be logical to assume that this wreck was called the Damsel. But this is only a guess.

### 170. British cargo steamship THALA
LOCATION:   57° 05′ 06″ N. 07° 13′ 36″ W.

The Thala was of 4399 tons gross, was built in 1928 and had dimensions of 370 × 52·3 × 25·9.

This vessel was on route from Pepl to Tees with a general cargo when she was wrecked at Hartamul, on South Uist on the Outer Hebrides, on 8th February 1941.

There is a report on Lloyd's List of 13th May 1970 which states '7–8 tons of brass and copper, value £3,000, have been salvaged from the Thala in April 1970'. A wreck of this size would certainly be worth diving on, even after salvage operations. Perhaps the salvage company could give you more details. After all, I should not think they would still be interested after removing that much cargo.

### 171. Unknown
LOCATION:   57° 05′ 42″ N. 07° 22′ 40″ W.

This wreck was first located in 1966. The only other information I have is that part of the superstructure dries at low water springs. Could be worth a visit, but after a glance at the charts I would say that you had better watch the tide tables rather carefully.

### 172. Collier ST BRANDON
LOCATION:   56° 40′ 36″ N. 06° 31′ 05″ W.

This is a good one for the wreck detective. All that is known is that the St Brandon was wrecked after being stranded 'on the reefs north of Rubba Mor Peninsula'. Unfortunately, the date is unknown except that it is 'approximately 1920'.

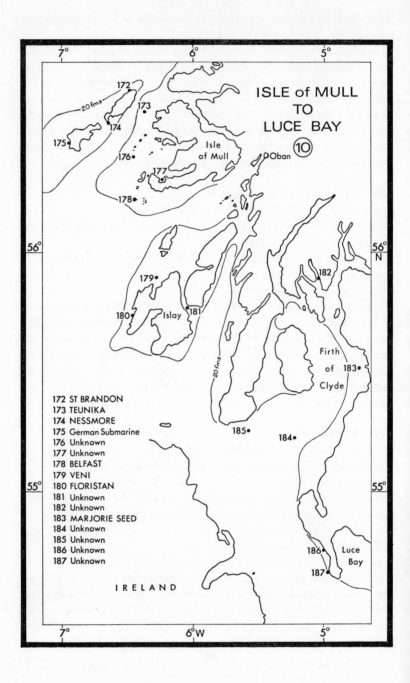

ISLE of MULL
TO
LUCE BAY
⑩

172 ST BRANDON
173 TEUNIKA
174 NESSMORE
175 German Submarine
176 Unknown
177 Unknown
178 BELFAST
179 VENI
180 FLORISTAN
181 Unknown
182 Unknown
183 MARJORIE SEED
184 Unknown
185 Unknown
186 Unknown
187 Unknown

### 173.  Dutch motor vessel TEUNIKA

LOCATION:    56° 35′ 40″ N. 06° 23′ 36″ W.

The Teunika, of 199 tons gross and with dimensions of 112 × 22 ×
8, vanished on 16th May 1969, with a cargo of gravel.

A report at the time of loss gave the position as '2½ miles 253°
from Caliach Point'. This position is assumed to be comparatively
accurate.

The location is between the Isle of Mull and the island of Coll--
an area not noted for good diving weather. Depths range from 100
to 200 feet.

### 174.  British cargo steamship NESSMORE

LOCATION:    56° 33′ 42″ N. 06° 41′ 24″ W.

This iron hulled vessel, of 3377 tons gross, 2216 tons net, was built
in 1882 by the Barrow Shipbuilding Company, and had dimensions
of 340 × 40·4 × 24·2—a considerable size by most standards.

While on route from Montreal to Liverpool with a general cargo of
cattle, cheese, apples, pit planks and stoves, the Nessmore ran
aground at Caroles Reef, south-east of (the records state 'Corr'
but I can find no such place name; it must be a misprint) Coll.

The wreck might be lying near the reef. It all depends on how
much buoyancy was in her when she slipped off the reef.

### 175.  German submarine

LOCATION:    56° 28′ 00″ N. 06° 59′ 00″ W.

This is an unconfirmed vessel, the story of which came about from
an indirect source.

In April 1970 a salvage firm, Messrs Arnold Young, asked the
Hydrographic Department if they had any information about a
German submarine that was captured in this area, taken in tow,
and later broke adrift while near the Island of Tiree.

The Hydrographic Department had no such information, but perhaps a little research could unearth some.

### 176.  Unknown

LOCATION:    56° 25′ 02″ N. 06° 29′ 42″ W.

This wreck was first located in 1922, and the position was confirmed
in 1952. The site is relatively near Staffa Island and the famous
Fingal's Cave.

The 1922 report states that 'two masts of the wreck are showing at

low water springs, 178° 595 yards from Hutcheson's Monument'.
The masts, of course, are no longer showing, but it could be an interesting wreck.

### 177. Unknown
LOCATION:  56° 19′ 20″ N. 06° 15′ 50″ W.

This wreck, tucked in a secluded bay in the southern part of the Isle of Mull, was first reported in 1943. There have been no further visits for confirmation.

The 1943 report only states that in this position there is a wreck 'with at least 12 feet of water over it'.

General depths are only 20 feet, so there probably will not be much left of the remains. On the other hand, the bay is relatively sheltered, and provided there is good access from land, or you have a good boat, it should make an easy and possibly interesting dive.

### 178. British steamship BELFAST
LOCATION:  56° 14′ 18″ N. 06° 27′ 39″ W.

This iron hulled vessel was of 1638 tons gross, 1293 tons net, and had dimensions of 265·6 × 33·3 × 24·3.

While on route from Sapele to Belfast, with a cargo of timber, the Belfast is reputed (I can find no definite reports) to have struck West Rock—which is apparently permanently submerged—off Iona. This was on 23rd March 1885.

Because of its age, this wreck would make an interesting dive. It must be worth looking for, because the depths around Iona, unlike many of the islands in this area, do not plunge to 200 feet plus almost immediately. Average depths, even some way off the west side, are between 20–60 feet, well within the limits for the average subaqua diver.

### 179. Norwegian motor vessel VENI
LOCATION:  55° 55′ 00″ N. 06° 18′ 00″ W.

This vessel, of 2982 tons gross, was in ballast when she was wrecked on Balach Rocks, north of Ard noamh, Islay, on 11th January 1948. The area, depthwise, is quite diveable, the deepest of the general depths being around 90 feet.

There is a report that 'a Mr Scott, a diver, has purchased the wreck'. The strange thing about this report is that it does not state that Mr Scott has found the wreck—only purchased it. So it could be that the Veni has not yet been found.

### 180.  British steamship FLORISTAN
LOCATION:    55° 45′ 00″ N. 06° 28′ 00″ W.
A big 'un. The Floristan was of 5478 tons gross, and was built in 1928.
While on route from Manchester to the Persian Gulf with a general cargo, the Floristan went ashore on 20th January 1942, approximately 6 miles north of Orsay Light near Kilchiaran Bay. And that's about all.
If no one has yet found it, this should make the perfect wreck for research. It is comparatively recent, a large vessel, and the depths average only 60 feet near shore and 120 feet offshore.

### 181.  Unknown
LOCATION:    55° 47′ 37″ N. 06° 03′ 49″ W.
This wreck was first located during a survey in 1933, and at that time the tips of the masts were showing at low water. Subsequent surveys have confirmed the position, but the masts are no longer visible.

### 182.  Unknown
LOCATION:    55° 55′ 08″ N. 05° 03′ 22″ W.
This wreck was first reported in 1954, and at that time the top dried at low water.
The latest report is by a diver, in 1966. According to him, it is a good shore dive, and the wreck seems to be that of a treble-screw motor minesweeper-type vessel, sunk approximately 20 years ago. The site is just off Bute Island.

### 183.  British cargo vessel MARJORIE SEED
LOCATION:    55° 32′ 12″ N. 04° 43′ 30″ W.
The Marjorie Seed was of 1860 tons gross, was built in 1907 by Osborne Graham and Company, and had dimensions of 279·3 × 40·1 × 18·1.
While on route from Glasgow to Helvie with a cargo of coal and coke, she foundered on 25th December 1924, '1½ miles 234° from the West Pier Light'.
The location is in the Firth of Clyde, west of Troon, in depths

ranging from 72 to 130 feet. Farther west, across the Clyde, lies the Isle of Arran, a popular holiday area for west coast Scots.

### 184. Unknown
LOCATION: 55° 14' 48" N. 05° 15' 10" W.
This is a fairly deep wreck, and is for experienced divers only.
First located in 1966, the position was confirmed in 1968. All that is known is that the remains stand some 15 feet high, in general depths of 154 feet.
The location is between the southern extremity of the peninsula of Kintyre and Girvan, on the mainland. Nearby is the famous island of Ailsa Craig.
If you want a really accurate fix, the Decca positions are: Red E 15·16, purple F 65·60.

### 185. Unknown
LOCATION: 55° 14' 48" N. 05° 15' 10" W.
This wreck was first located in 1952, and further surveys in 1953 and 1968 have confirmed the position.
The surveys report that 'it is a large rust-coloured wreck, lying on its side, and very prominent when viewed from east or west'.
The location is off the south side of Kintyre, near Sanda Island. Be careful, though, there are nasty races to the west of the island.

### 186. Unknown
LOCATION: 54° 44' 53" N. 04° 59' 19" W.
Lying on the western side of the peninsula that terminates in the Mull of Galloway, this wreck is close inshore.
It was first located by a diver, Mr Jessop, in 1966. According to his report, 'the wreck is close to shore, and may be that of a light ship'. That's all—but it should be easy to find.

### 187. Unknown
LOCATION: 54° 40' 09" N. 04° 57' 57" W.
This wreck was first reported by the same Mr Jessop who discovered Wreck 186. The site is farther to the south of the previous wreck.
Mr Jessop only reported that there was a wreck in this position, and that he had found the name 'Cragsman' on the remains. Unfortunately it is not known exactly where he found the name of

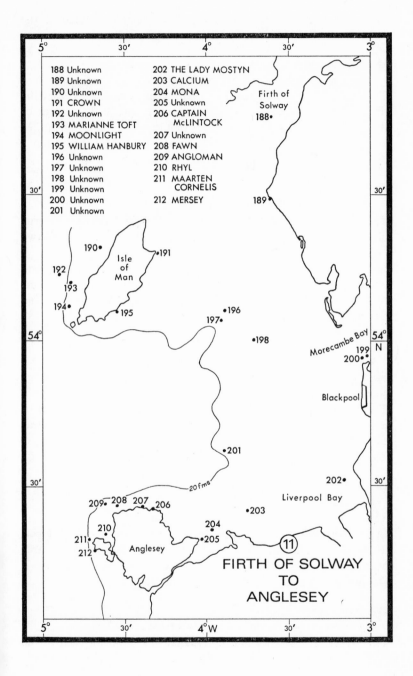

188 Unknown
189 Unknown
190 Unknown
191 CROWN
192 Unknown
193 MARIANNE TOFT
194 MOONLIGHT
195 WILLIAM HANBURY
196 Unknown
197 Unknown
198 Unknown
199 Unknown
200 Unknown
201 Unknown

202 THE LADY MOSTYN
203 CALCIUM
204 MONA
205 Unknown
206 CAPTAIN McLINTOCK
207 Unknown
208 FAWN
209 ANGLOMAN
210 RHYL
211 MAARTEN CORNELIS
212 MERSEY

Firth of Solway

188•

189•

190•
•191
Isle of Man
192•
193•
194•
195•

196•
197•
•198
Morecambe Bay
199••
200••

Blackpool

•201

20 fms

202•
Liverpool Bay

209•
208•
207•
206•
•203
210•
204•
•205
211•
212•
Anglesey

⑪

54°

30'

54° N

30'

5°   30'   4°   30'   3°

FIRTH OF SOLWAY
TO
ANGLESEY

the wreck, and whether this could have been the name of the vessel. A good one for the wreck detective.

### 188. Unknown
LOCATION: 54° 06′ 00″ N. 04° 32′ 49″ W.

This wreck was first reported in 1910, when it was stated that the masts were visible at low water. A recent report in the records of the Hydrographic Department states that they are still visible at low water. I have not visited this site in the Firth of Solway, but I doubt if that is still the case, after all this time.

### 189. Unknown
LOCATION: 54° 29′ 19″ N. 03° 36′ 46″ W.

The first record of this wreck was in 1960, and stated that part of the wreck dried at low water springs, and that there were two boilers, a vertical spar, and further wreckage.

It is reputed to be the remains of a Spanish ship which grounded many years ago, then slipped back into the water. Apparently, the remains were originally scheduled for salvage, but there is no record of any salvage ever taking place.

### 190. Unknown
LOCATION: 54° 19′ 00″ N. 04° 39′ 00″ W.

First reported in 1940. The report only stated that 'the wreckage consists, among other things, of an aircraft engine'.

There is nothing else I can trace on file. So, is this what is left of the wreck of an aircraft, or is it the remains of a vessel that was carrying aero engines?

The depth is in the region of 60 feet.

### 191. Steam trawler CROWN
LOCATION: 54° 18′ 00″ N. 04° 18′ 30″ W.

This trawler, of 266 tons gross, was built in 1906.

In the November of the same year, it was fishing out of Fleetwood, foundered, and was wrecked off the Isle of Man near Maughold Head.

Depths in this area are rarely more than 30 feet.

### 192. Unknown
LOCATION: 54° 13′ 40″ N. 04° 54′ 00″ W.

This wreck was first located in 1969. It lies some way out to the west of Craig Rock, which is off the west coast of the Isle of Man. Nothing else is known, except that the depth is about 120 feet. The underwater visibility in this area can be remarkably clear, so it must be worth a visit.

### 193. Danish steamship MARIANNE TOFT
LOCATION:   54° 12′ 00″ N. 04° 50′ 00″ W.

This steamship was of 2302 tons gross, was built in 1930, and had dimensions of 282·8 × 42 × 17·8.

While on route from Oxelosund to Barrow with a cargo of iron ore, the Marianne Toft collided with the Cornelius Ford, and sank about 9 miles north of 'The Chickens'. This was on 12th September 1945.

The location is just inside the 20 fathom line, so the wreck should be in a depth somewhere between 60–80 feet. It is highly unlikely that she drifted over the 20 fathom line—with such a cargo she must have gone down like a stone.

### 194. British motor vessel MOONLIGHT
LOCATION:   54° 07′ 15″ N. 04° 50′ 00″ W.

With a gross tonnage of 200 tons, the Moonlight was built in 1961 and had dimensions of 117·8 × 25·3 × 8·5. She was registered at Greenock, and was owned, at the time of loss, by the Light Shipping Co. Ltd.

While on route on 9th September 1970, with a cargo of salt, she capsized and sank after the cargo shifted in heavy seas. Two of the crew of four were lost.

Depths in the area of sinking average 110 feet.

### 195. British steam trawler WILLIAM HANBURY
LOCATION:   54° 06′ 00″ N. 04° 32′ 49″ W.

This trawler, of 204 tons gross, was stranded off St Anne's Head in 1942. I have heard that the wreck has been located, but nothing definite.

### 196. Unknown
LOCATION:   54° 06′ 30″ N. 03° 53′ 20″ W.

This wreck was first located after fishermen had repeatedly lost trawls. But I do not know the date on which it was found.

The Decca position is: Red 16·00 B. Green 30·00 H. The depth is about 100 feet.

## 197. Unknown
LOCATION: 54° 04′ 20″ N. 03° 54′ 25″ W.

This wreck is similar to Wreck 196 in that it was first discovered after fishing boats had repeatedly lost trawls. There is no further information.

The Decca position is: Red 19·50 B. Green 35·00 H. Depths, again, average 100 feet.

## 198. Unknown
LOCATION: 54° 00′ 15″ N. 03° 42′ 45″ W.

The story here is exactly the same as for Wrecks 196 and 197, except that depths average less at 70 feet.

The Decca position is: Red 17·30 B. Green 38·60 I.

## 199. Unknown
LOCATION: 53° 57′ 02″ N. 03° 01′ 12″ W.

This wreck was first reported in 1966. According to local information it is the remains of a fishing vessel that foundered and came ashore, then slipped back into the sea.

## 200. Unknown
LOCATION: 53° 56′ 43″ N. 03° 03′ 06″ W.

This wreck was first reported in 1966. The only other information I have is that it is a large wreck, and that the top dries slightly at low water springs.

I find it difficult to believe that the name of such an accessible wreck remains a mystery; local clubs must have dived on it many times. On the other hand, these waters are noted for poor visibility, so perhaps this is the reason.

## 201. Unknown
LOCATION: 53° 37′ 33″ N. 03° 53′ 16″ W.

The only information I have about this wreck is that it was discovered after many fishermen had reported lost trawls. It is inside—just—the 20 fathom line in average depths of 130 feet.

There is a possibility that this is the wreck of the Mona (see Wreck 204). The Decca position is: Red 23·5 O. Green 34·50 B.

## 202. British steamer THE LADY MOSTYN

LOCATION: 53° 31′ 20″ N. 03° 09′ 55″ W.

Of 305 tons gross, The Lady Mostyn vanished on 23rd July 1970, and is presumed to have struck a mine. The area of loss is approximately 79° 1½ miles from the Formby Light Vessel, and is just north of the Great Burbo Bank. The depths are generally very shallow, but the poor underwater visibility of Liverpool Bay will probably ensure that the wreck is never found.

## 203. British steamer CALCIUM

LOCATION: 53° 25′ 00″ N. 03° 45′ 00″ W.

This is a war-time casualty about which very little is known. The Calcium was mined and sunk on 30th December 1940.
The area is slightly north of the Constable Banks, with average depths of 50 feet.

## 204. British steamship MONA

LOCATION: 53° 21′ 00″ N. 03° 57′ 55″ W.

The Mona was of 207 tons gross, and was built in 1902.
While on route from Garston to Dublin with a cargo of coal, she foundered and sank off Puffin Island on 17th November 1916.
The water surrounding Puffin Island ranges in depth from drying at low water to 35 feet. Unfortunately, the presence of the muddy Menai Strait ensures that the visibility is invariably nil—or very nearly so.

## 205. Unknown

LOCATION: 53° 19′ 04″ N. 04° 01′ 50″ W.

First located in 1960, this is a large wreck. The 1960 survey reported that the wreck dried two feet at low water springs, but I do not know if this is still the case.
The area is north-west of Puffin Island, and the bearing and distance is: 46½° 4·5 cables from Trwyn du Light.

## 206. British iron steamer CAPTAIN McLINTOCK

LOCATION: 53° 25′ 06″ N. 04° 19′ 42″ W.

Of 267 tons gross, the Captain McLintock was built in 1863 and had dimensions of 154·2 × 22·3 × 10·5.
While on route from Garston to Dublin with a cargo of coal, she foundered and sank close inshore off Amlwych, on 9th December 1886.

### 207. Unknown

LOCATION:   53° 25′ 50″ N. 04° 23′ 24″ W.

Another wreck lying close inshore. But beware, the coastline here dips into depths of 110 feet, and it is here that a wreck of unknown name resides.

### 208. British steamship FAWN

LOCATION:   53° 26′ 06″ N. 04° 32′ 30″ W.

The Fawn was of 300 tons gross, was built in 1884 and had dimensions of 145·5 × 23·1 × 10·7.

While on route from Llanelly to Liverpool with a cargo of coal, the Fawn was wrecked on 14th December 1886.

The area of loss averages 70 feet of depth. Also in the area is the wreck of the Lord Athlumney (see *Shipwrecks Around Britain*).

### 209. British steamship ANGLOMAN

LOCATION:   53° 26′ 30″ N. 04° 36′ 30″ W.

The Angloman was a largish vessel of 4892 tons gross, and had dimensions of 403·5 × 45·6 × 25.

While on route from Boston to Liverpool with a cargo of cattle, grain and provisions, she was wrecked on the Skerries Rock in February 1897.

The Skerries Rock juts out of the sea off Carmel Head, and the surrounding waters quickly dip to 90 feet in depth. This is also the site of the wreck of the Castilian, as described in *Shipwrecks Around Britain*.

### 210. British steamship RHYL

LOCATION:   53° 20′ 00″ N. 04° 37′ 00″ W.

The Rhyl was a 'middleweight' of 1274 tons gross, and was built by Palmers Shipbuilding Company in 1879. She had dimensions of 240 × 33·2 × 19·3, and was owned, at the time of loss, by John Cory and Sons. While on route from Ardrossan to Newport, in ballast, she collided with the steamer Royston Grange on 24th July 1900, and sank off Holyhead.

The depth of water in the location given is only about 20 feet, but she could have easily drifted slightly to the west, into 70 feet.

### 211.   Dutch fishing vessel MAARTEN CORNELIS
LOCATION:   53° 18′ 54″ N. 14° 43′ 18″ W.

The Maarten Cornelis foundered and sank on 19th March 1971, after striking the rocks of the South Stack.

The location is the one given by the Superintendent of Trinity House at Holyhead, at the time of loss. The position is just inside the 20 fathom line, and if this is correct the wreck is in 120 feet of water. However, it is possible that it lies slightly west, in the Holyhead Deep. In this case the remains will probably never be found or visited, because the Deep has a depth of 240 feet.

The Decca Chain position is: 3B Red F 7·30. Green A 42·00.

### 212.   British iron steamship MERSEY
LOCATION:   53° 17′ 00″ N. 04° 41′ 15″ W.

The Mersey was of 342 tons gross, with dimensions of 159·2 × 23·7 × 10·3.

While on route from Newport to Liverpool, she was stranded at Penrhos Point Rocks on 31st July 1886, and became a total loss. The area of loss is close inshore, but the underwater terrain quickly dips into depths of 90 feet plus.

### 213.   British submarine H5
LOCATION:   53° 04′ 00″ N. 04° 40′ 00″ W.

This was an 'H' class Hl-type British submarine, built in 1915 by Vickers of Montreal, Canada. She had a surface displacement of 364 tons, and an underwater displacement of 434 tons, and had dimensions of $150\frac{1}{4}$ × $50\frac{3}{4}$ (beam). The diesel engines powered two screws, providing a surface speed of 13 knots, and an underwater speed of 10 knots. The bow contained 4 × 18 torpedo tubes. The complement or crew was 22.

The records only state that the H5 was 'sunk by collision on 6th March 1918'.

Perhaps some wreck detective would like to follow this up. What, for instance, was the name of the ship the H5 was in collision with?

### 214.   Unknown (two wrecks)
LOCATION:   52° 51′ 02″ N. 04° 43′ 36·5″ W.

This is on the northern side of the Lleyn Peninsula—very good but rugged diving. Nearby Penrallt was the site of an excellent

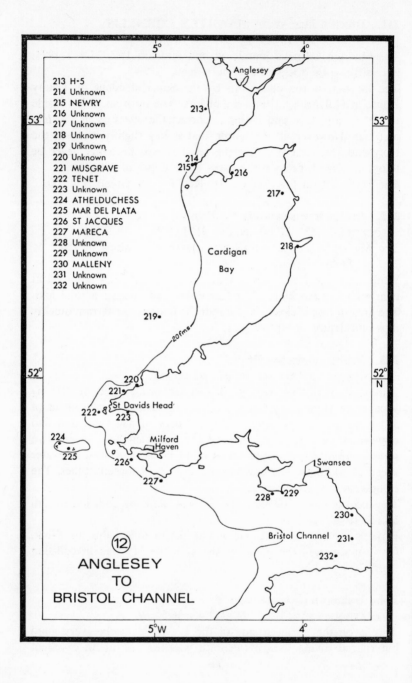

213 H-5
214 Unknown
215 NEWRY
216 Unknown
217 Unknown
218 Unknown
219 Unknown
220 Unknown
221 MUSGRAVE
222 TENET
223 Unknown
224 ATHELDUCHESS
225 MAR DEL PLATA
226 ST JACQUES
227 MARECA
228 Unknown
229 Unknown
230 MALLENY
231 Unknown
232 Unknown

Anglesey

213•

214•
215•          •216

          •217

Cardigan

Bay
                    218•

219•
~20 fms~

220•
221•
222•  •    St Davids Head
      223

224 •
225•          Milford
          Haven
  226•                          Swansea
      227•
                  228•  •229
                              230•
      ⑫                  Bristol Channel  231•
  ANGLESEY                        232•
      TO
BRISTOL CHANNEL

diving centre a few years ago. Unfortunately, it has virtually closed down, but I hear that someone is taking an interest in re-opening it. Off Fair Island lies the cargo of an un-named iron carrying schooner; and on the rocks at Penrallt there is the wreck of a smuggler, well buried in the sand. Both are well dived on—but as far as I know they are still mysteries.

### 215. NEWRY
LOCATION: 52° 51' 00" N. 04° 43' 54" W.

This vessel, of approximately 500 tons, was on route from Newry to Quebec with about 3–400 immigrants when she ran into bad weather and struck shore, close to Maen Lellt, on 19th April 1830. So it's an old one that would make a very interesting find. All the crew were saved, but 60–70 of the immigrants were lost. As so many people survived, there should be ample records.

Depths in the recorded area of loss are only about 25 feet. But you do not have to go far out to be in 100 feet of water—and the 20 fathom line is not far from this.

### 216. Unknown
LOCATION: 52° 48' 51" N. 04° 29' 14" W.

This 'item' is listed as 'obstruction, wreck'. Nothing more is known. Is it a wreck? Or just an obstruction such as a rock?

The site is near the attractive harbour town of Abersoch, in Tremadoch Bay. Depths in the bay are very shallow, and if this is a wreck it is probably mostly buried in the sands.

### 217. Unknown
LOCATION: 52° 44' 15" N. 04° 18' 16" W.

This wreck was first located in 1969. The survey reported that it was fairly substantial, about 8 feet high, in general depths of 30 feet.

The nearest town is Barmouth, which could be used as a base for an expedition.

### 218. Unknown (three wrecks)
LOCATION: 52° 31' 36" N. 04° 02' 26" W.

Three wrecks—old ones at that— for the price or effort of one! This is a most intriguing site. Very little is known about these wrecks despite the fact that they were first recorded in 1890! The positions were confirmed as recently as 1969.

The area is very shallow, and at least one of the wrecks dries at low water. It seems incredible that so little is known about them when they are so accessible. The records do not state how it is known that there are in fact three wrecks—only that they are there.

### 219. Unknown

LOCATION: 52° 14′ 39″ N. 04° 58′ 30″ W.

A big one—but deep. This wreck was first located in World War One by the Escort Group No. 5. The report stated: 'The wreck is in position 260° lying north–south. It is a very large wreck, standing some 40 feet high on the sea bed'.

The position was confirmed by a 1971 survey, by which time part of the wreck had obviously collapsed. The latter report stated: 'The wreck is only 20 feet high, and 230 feet in length, in general depths of 158 feet'. The length and original height might give some wreck detective an idea of the name of the wreck.

### 220. Unknown

LOCATION: 51° 57′ 36″ N. 05° 07′ 30″ W.

This wreck was first located in 1968, by a diver. His report stated: 'The wreck lies alongside an underwater cliff and is about 15 feet high—some metal rises a further 6 feet or so. There is evidence of salvage work'.

The location is in Abercastle Bay, 4·65 miles SE by S of Strumble Light.

### 221. British iron steamship MUSGRAVE

LOCATION: 51° 56′ 55″ N. 05° 12′ 20″ W.

This was a vessel of 252 tons gross, was built in 1871, and had dimensions of 130·7 × 21·9 × 10·5.

While on route from Britain Ferry to Dundalk with a cargo of coal, she ran on to Stedge Rock, 1 mile west of Pan Clegyr Point (about 5 miles west of Strumble Head) on 25th November 1892, and became a total loss.

### 222. British steamship TENET

LOCATION: 51° 52′ 00″ N. 05° 11′ 45″ W.

The Tenet was a steel vessel of 603 tons gross, was built in 1910 and had dimensions of 186·8 × 28·7 × 11·8.

No one knows how the Tenet sank. She just vanished on 25th October 1912, while on route from Newport to Londonderry with a cargo of coal.

Depths in the area average about 100 feet.

### 223. Unknown

LOCATION: 51° 52' 00" N. 05° 11' 45" W.

This wreck lies close inshore in St David's Bay, on the north side.

Just inside the harbour, on Black Rock, are the remains of an old sailing ship. It is said locally that it is a wooden ship, wrecked about 1850.

I understand that it is quite a popular wreck with divers—perhaps one of them has uncovered a lead as to its identity. According to one dive report, there are plenty of timber frames still visible, and pieces of ironwork, with, of course, many snagged anchors.

### 224. British tanker ATHELDUCHESS

LOCATION: 51° 44' 02" N. 05° 39' 00" W.

The Athelduchess was a large vessel of 8940 tons gross, built in 1929, with dimensions of 475 × 63·3 × 35. The owner at the time of loss was the Athel Line of London.

There are two treacherous groups of rock lying out at sea from St David's Bay, and it was the farthest group—the Smalls—that the Athelduchess ran on to and broke in two. The stern half, which included the engines, was floated off the rocks and towed into Milford Haven. It was subsequently purchased by the Ministry of Transport. (I wonder, did they only purchase half a boat!) The fore part, which included the bridge, slipped back into the water.

The site is not exactly easy of access, but if the remains are in the immediate vicinity of the Smalls it should be worth a visit. On the other hand, if the fore part drifted a little before sinking, it could be in very deep water. It does not take long to find 120 feet off the north side, and 180 feet off the south.

### 225. Spanish steamer MAR DEL PLATA

LOCATION: 51° 43' 00" N. 05° 35' 00" W.

The Mar Del Plata was of 1191 tons gross, was built in 1919 by Soc. Anon. Astilleros Del Nervion, and had dimensions of 231·6 × 31 × 13·5.

While on route from Clyde to Bilbao with a cargo of coal, this vessel vanished on 30th January 1923, in a position that should have been, according to reports, in the area of the Hats and Barrels Rocks—which lie to the east of the Smalls (see Wreck 224). The Barrels are particularly conspicuous because they dry about 10 feet at low water springs. Surrounding depths are about 130 feet.

### 226.  French steamer ST JAQUES
LOCATION :   51° 40′ 00″ N. 05° 10′ 00″ W.

This steel vessel of 2459 tons gross, 1339 tons net, with two decks, was built in 1909 by Ateliers & Chankes and had dimensions of 288·8 × 38·9 × 16·6.

A war-time casualty, the St Jaques was torpedoed by a German submarine and sank on 15th September 1917.

The area of loss was reported as just off St Anne's Head, in the mouth of the approaches to Milford Haven. Depths average around 30 feet.

### 227.  British cargo ship MARECA
LOCATION :   51° 35′ 00″ N. 04° 58′ 00″ W.

The Mareca was a vessel of 2211 tons gross, was built by Palmers Co in 1882, and had dimensions of 311·2 × 37·3 × 23.

While on route from Cork to Newport, in ballast, she sank somewhere west of St Govan's Head on 21st January 1898.

All the crew—I do not know how many—were saved. Six of them were found in one of the boats, and one of the occupants, second mate T. Scorer, stated that the Mareca left Queenstown and experienced heavy weather in the Channel. At night, in dense fog, she struck the Welsh coast at a speed of 2–3 knots. The bottom was ripped open and water rushing in caused the boilers to explode. It was difficult to get the two boats down in the heavy swell, but they succeeded eventually, and landed nearby at St Govan's Head.

### 228.  Unknown (3 wrecks)
LOCATION :   51° 32′ 09″ N. 04° 12′ 36″ W.

In this area, off St Govan's Head, there are at least three recorded wrecks on my files. I have no statistical information—only names and dates.

The steamer Blue Bell was wrecked on 15th February 1913; the steamer Carew Castle in 1932; and the steamer Epidauro in 1913. The depths average from 30 to 130 feet, and there are nasty races all around. These are usually marked on charts.

### 229.  Unknown (5 wrecks)
LOCATION:   51° 32′ 30″ N. 04° 08′ 40″ W.
The area around Oxwich Point has five entries in my files, but I am sure there are many more wrecks than this.
The steamer Merthyr foundered on the Point in 1913; the steamer Nanset in 1916; the sailing vessel Primrose in 1920; the tug Mumbles in 1931; and the British sailing vessel Tridonia, of 2168 tons gross, was on route from Dublin to Buenos Aires, in ballast when she sank here on 29th October 1916.
Depths average 25 to 100 feet several hundred yards out.

### 230.  Sailing ship MALLENY
LOCATION:   51° 27′ 00″ N. 03° 40′ 00″ W.
This would be an interesting find because the Malleny was an iron sailing ship. She was of 1053 tons gross, was built by T. Royden and Sons in 1868, and had dimensions of 204·7 × 34·8 × 20·9. The owner at the time of loss was Hughs and Co.
While on route from Cardiff to Rio de Janeiro with a cargo of coal, the Malleny was wrecked on Tuskar Rock on 15th October 1886.

### 231.  Unknown
LOCATION:  51° 21′ 00″ N. 03° 39′ 47″ W.
This is not necessarily a precise location. It was given me by an old diving friend who located the wreck while on holiday.

### 232.  Unknown
LOCATION:   51° 16′ 55″ N. 03° 46′ 47″ W.
This wreck, in 75 feet, was located in 1949.

### 233.  British steamship NORTHFIELD
LOCATION:   50° 59′ 00″ N. 04° 37′ 00″ W.
The Northfield was a vessel of 2099 tons gross, was built in 1901 and had dimensions of 288·5 × 48 × 18·5.

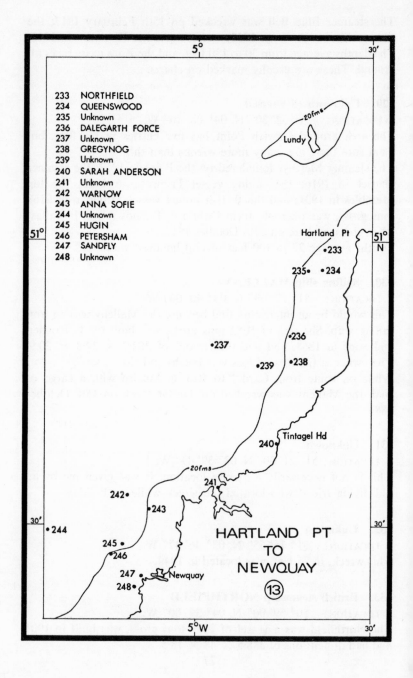

233 NORTHFIELD
234 QUEENSWOOD
235 Unknown
236 DALEGARTH FORCE
237 Unknown
238 GREGYNOG
239 Unknown
240 SARAH ANDERSON
241 Unknown
242 WARNOW
243 ANNA SOFIE
244 Unknown
245 HUGIN
246 PETERSHAM
247 SANDFLY
248 Unknown

Lundy

20fms

Hartland Pt
•233

235• •234

•236

•237
•239  •238

Tintagel Hd
240•

20fms
241•

242•
•243

•244

245•
•246

247•
248•  Newquay

HARTLAND PT
TO
NEWQUAY
⑬

She was torpedoed by a German submarine on 3rd March 1918, and sank on that date with the loss of 16 lives.

There were several reports on the sinking. The captain of a patrol vessel in the area at the time gave the position above. One of the survivors stated that the Northfield was on her way up the Bristol Channel '5 miles from land' at the time. A gunner said that they were '25 miles south-west of Lundy'. All agreed that the Northfield sank at once, and this no doubt was why so many lives were lost.

### 234.  British merchant steamship QUEENSWOOD
LOCATION:   50° 57′ 00″ N. 04° 38′ 00″ W.

The Queenswood was a vessel of 2071 tons gross.

She was captured by a German submarine on 16th February 1917, 6 miles south-west from Hartland Point. The submarine then sank the Queenswood with gunfire. I am not sure whether the submarine gave the crew the option of leaving the vessel first, but it seems likely that this was the case.

The assumed site of sinking lies inside the 20 fathom line, in which case the wreck should reside in less than 120 feet of water.

### 235.  Unknown
LOCATION:   50° 57′ 00″ N. 04° 41′ 15″ W.

This is a very large wreck which was located by the Escort Group No. 9 during World War Two.

The remains are lying in a 023° × 203° direction, are 225 feet in length and stand some 36 feet high—big by most standards.

This section of coast can be very dangerous, because it is exposed to the force of the Atlantic, but with care this wreck should be well worth a look at. With such a length, and the known angle of lie, it should not be too difficult to locate.

### 236.  British merchant ship DALEGARTH FORCE
LOCATION:   50° 50′ 00″ N. 04° 44′ 00″ W.

This was a vessel of 684 tons gross, was built in 1914 and had dimensions of 175 × 28 × 11.

The Dalegarth Force was torpedoed and sunk by a German submarine on 18th April 1918. 5 lives were lost.

There are three reports relating to the sinking on my files—all from survivors. The master's report gave the location shown above;

another states 'we went down immediately, 12 miles south-west of Hartland Point'; and the final report only states that 'the ship went down in 3 minutes'.

If the position given is accurate, and the vessel did go down immediately, then the wreck should be in about 100 feet or less of water. But this position is very near the 20 fathom line, and the remains might be much deeper.

## 237. Unknown
LOCATION:    50° 49′ 00″ N. 04° 57′ 42″ W.

This is a large wreck, in deep water. It lies beyond the 20 fathom line, in about 150 feet of water. There is a terse entry in the records of the Hydrographic Department which states that the wreck 'stands 35 feet high on the sea bed, and is 150 feet in length'. The length would indicate that the wreck is not 'on end', and with a height of 35 feet it must be a large vessel indeed. The only other information is that the wreck was first located 'during World War Two'—I don't know who by.

## 238. British steamship GREGYNOG
LOCATION:    50° 47′ 00″ N. 04° 43′ 15″ W.

This vessel was of 1701 tons gross, 1048 tons net, was built in 1899 by S. P. Austin and Sons of Sunderland, and had dimensions of 268·3 × 37·7 × 17. The owner at the time of loss was Lambton and Helton.

The Gregynog was carrying a cargo of 2365 tons of coal when she was torpedoed and sank on 18th April 1918. Three lives were lost. The position given above is based on the message the master gave at the time of sinking, which was 'about 3 miles offshore, 16 miles south-west of Hartland Point'. This position, however approximate, is at least well inside the 20 fathom line and as such is at least worth a search.

## 239. Unknown
LOCATION:    50° 46′ 54″ N. 04° 49′ 12″ W.

This wreck lies to the north of Tintagel Head, on the wrong side of the 20 fathom line. It was first located by a survey ship following complaints from fishermen who had lost their nets.

The Decca position is: Green G 32·3. Purple E 78·9.

### 240.  Barque SARAH ANDERSON
LOCATION:   50° 38′ 30″ N. 04° 46′ 00″ W.

The Sarah Anderson was a vessel of 589 tons gross, was built in 1865 and had dimensions of 173 × 28 × 18.

While on route from Coquimbo to Fleetwood with a cargo of manganese ore dye, she foundered off Boscastle and sank on 17th October 1886. There were no survivors.

Although not a large wreck by most standards, the age of the vessel makes her historically interesting. The site is close inshore and should not be too difficult to locate. One—unconfirmed—report of that time stated that the vessel was wrecked on Gull Rock.

### 241.  Unknown
LOCATION:   50° 33′ 43·5″ N. 04° 56′ 08″ W.

Even a snorkel diver could visit this wreck—and perhaps clear up a mystery.

The wreck was first discovered in 1967, and the position has since been confirmed. It lies in very shallow water—in fact the top dries partly at low water springs.

An unconfirmed report states that the wreck is 'quite old, and sank about the turn of the century'. A French brigantine, the Angele, sank in this area in 1911, so this is one possibility. In such an accessible site, I am sure it will not be too long before someone identifies the remains.

### 242.  British merchant steamship WARNOW
LOCATION:   50° 33′ 00″ N. 05° 11′ 30″ W.

The Warnow was of 1953 tons gross, was built by B. J. Redhead and Company, and had dimensions of 257 × 34·7 × 19·6. The owner at the time of the loss was J. Mitchell and Sons.

On 2nd May 1917, she was torpedoed and sank just off Trevose Head. This is an approximation, because in the hurry to abandon the ship no proper fix was taken; or at least, none was reported later.

The area of loss is outside the 20 fathom line, and because the vessel sank in a reasonably short space of time it is unlikely that she drifted into shallower water.

### 243.  Armed British merchant steamship ANNA SOFIE
LOCATION:   50° 31′ 42″ N. 05° 08′ 05″ W.

This vessel was of 2577 tons gross, 1609 tons net, was built in

1896 by B. Roper and Sons of Stockton, and had dimensions of 320·2 × 44 × 20·7. She was built of steel, had one deck, and was owned at the time of loss by Wm. France Fenwick and Company. Where is she? Well, the only report as to position was '4 miles west of Trevose Head'. The Padstow Coastguard reported that the vessel sank in 30 minutes. Now bear in mind that if possible the Anna Sofie would have tried for land before sinking. How much ground (or rather, water) do you think she made up before she went down? On the other hand, perhaps she could not manoeuvre. In which case, which way was the tide running!!

## 244. Unknown
LOCATION: 50° 29' 20" N. 05° 25' 17" W.

This is another wreck that was first drawn attention to when fishermen started losing trawls. Nothing else is known about it. It was first reported in 1969. In this area, HMS Warwick was lost on 20th February 1944. Could this be the one?

The Decca position is: Green J 43·0. Purple D 66·4.

## 245. Swedish cargo steamer HUGIN
LOCATION: 50° 28' 00" N. 05° 12' 00" W.

This was a vessel of 1666 tons gross, 1003 tons net, was built by Mackie Thompson of Glasgow in 1889, and had dimensions of 260 × 36·7 × 16·6. She was built of steel, with one deck, and the owner at the time of loss was Angf. Svithoid of Sweden.

The Hugin was torpedoed by a German submarine, and sank on 21st February 1918. One report said that the wreck occurred '5 miles NNW of Newquay'. The master of the ship gave a slightly different and more informative statement, 'torpedoed 4½ miles off St Agnes, and foundered one hour later'.

The area of loss is just outside the 20 fathom line, in depths averaging 120–150 feet. But which way did the Hugin drift for one hour?

## 246. British cargo ship PETERSHAM
LOCATION: 50° 27' 00" N. 05° 14' 00" W.

A substantial vessel, the Petersham was of 3381 tons gross, and had dimensions of 339 × 46·1 × 24·7.

While on route from Bilbao to Clyde with a cargo of iron ore, the Petersham was in collision with a vessel named the Serra, and sank approximately 10 miles south-west of Trevose Head.

The area of loss is just inside the 20 fathom line, but of course she could have drifted into deeper water before sinking. On the other hand, the wreck could be nearer land. Perhaps the report of the Serra—if anyone can locate it—could tell us more. One thing is certain. With such a heavy cargo it is unlikely that the sinking ship drifted far.

### 247.  SANDFLY
LOCATION:   50° 24′ 30″ N. 05° 09′ 00″ W.

Very little information is available about this vessel, except that she was in ballast and foundered on the west side of Kelsey Head, close to shore. This was on 25th September 1920.

The area is quite near Newquay, so it should be useful as a holiday/expedition.

### 248.  Unknown
LOCATION:   50° 23′ 30″ N. 05° 10′ 00″ W.

This wreck was first reported on 30th September 1918, when some naval officers at Penzance tendered the information that a wreck lay '3–4 cables W by N½N off Carter's Rocks'. At that time the 'mast of a small vessel' was showing about 3 feet at low tide. The mast has long since vanished, but the wreck—or what remains of it—is still there.

This site is also near Newquay, which would make a base for searching for this and Wreck 247.

### 249.  Armed British merchant steamer DUNDEE
LOCATION:   50° 22′ 00″ N. 05° 36′ 00″ W.

This vessel was of 2290 tons gross.

While on route from London to Swansea, she was torpedoed by a German submarine and sank on 31st January 1917, with the loss of one life.

The approximate location by survivors is 10 miles N by W from St Ives Head. This is beyond the 20 fathom line, so the wreck should be in 120–150 feet of water.

### 250.  British merchant steamship ST GEORGE
LOCATION:   50° 19′ 54″ N. 05° 18′ 06″ W.

The St George was a vessel of 548 tons gross, was built by the

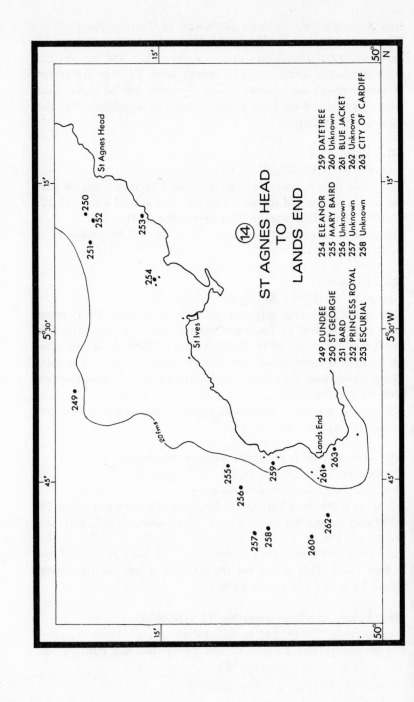

ST AGNES HEAD
TO
LANDS END

14

St Agnes Head

St Ives

Lands End

20 fms

249 DUNDEE
250 ST GEORGIE
251 BARD
252 PRINCESS ROYAL
253 ESCURIAL

254 ELEANOR
255 MARY BAIRD
256 Unknown
257 Unknown
258 Unknown

259 DATETREE
260 Unknown
261 BLUE JACKET
262 Unknown
263 CITY OF CARDIFF

London and Glasgow SB Company, and had dimensions of 190·5 × 28·9 × 13. She was owned at the time of loss by Murray Bros. While on route from Swansea to Nantes, via Bristol, with a cargo of copper bars and coal, she foundered and sank on 29th November 1882, about 4 miles north of Gull Rock.

Gull Rock lies midway between St Agnes Head and the 20 fathom line. The surrounding area averages about 100 feet in depth. If you see a diving group in the area, it is more than likely that they are looking for the St George. I do not suppose this would be because of the copper in the cargo?

### 251. Norwegian steamship BARD
LOCATION: 50° 19′ 30″ N. 05° 21′ 50″ W.

This is a double mystery.

The Bard was a vessel of 709 tons gross, 399 tons net, was built in 1892 by Nylands Vaerks, and had dimensions of 186·3 × 28·9 × 13·6.

On 11th December 1917, while carrying a cargo of coal and fire bricks, the Bard was torpedoed by a German submarine and sank. The following year, a report stated that the top of the wreck was visible at low tide. By the description of the remains, in particular the mast, it was obvious that the vessel could not be that of the Bard. So what is the name of this mystery vessel? And where is the Bard?

### 252. British merchant steamship PRINCESS ROYAL
LOCATION: 50° 19′ 20″ N. 05° 18′ 40″ W.

The Princess Royal was of 1986 tons gross, 866 tons net, was built in 1912 by Caledon SB Eng. Dundee, and had dimensions of 291·4 × 38·2 × 14·1. Built in steel, with two decks, she was owned at the time of loss by M. Longlands and Sons of Glasgow.

On 26th May 1918, while carrying a general cargo, she was torpedoed and sunk by a German submarine. 19 lives were lost, but the captain survived. In his report he stated that the ship sank about 3 miles WNW from St Agnes Head, and went down at once after being struck by the torpedo.

### 253. British cargo steamship ESCURIAL
LOCATION: 50° 15′ 48″ N. 05° 18′ 03″ W.

This was a Glasgow collier iron screwed schooner rigged as a

85

steamer. The vessel was of 1188 tons gross, 755 tons net, was built in 1879 and had dimensions of 230·2 × 30·2 × 22.

While on route from Cardiff to Fiume with a cargo of coal, the Escurial apparently sprang a leak after a collision with a Welsh pilot cutter. In heavy seas she was driven ashore on to Gull Sands. midway between Gull Rock and the Great West Headland. 14 lives were lost, including the captain. This was on 30th January 1895. Later, she slipped back into deeper water.

### 254. British cargo steamship ELEANOR
LOCATION:   50° 15′ 00″ N. 05° 24′ 48″ W.

The Eleanor was of 1277 tons gross, 767 tons net, was built in 1912 and had dimensions of 229·5 × 35·7 × 17.

While on route from Barry to Lisbon with a cargo of coal, the Eleanor lost a prop in a gale. After a while she drifted on to The Stones, near Godrevy, and on 22nd December 1922 became a total loss.

The Stones dry at low tide—19 feet at low water springs—and general depths range from 25 feet on the west side to 60 feet on the east. Admiralty Chart 2565 shows a wreck on the south-west of The Stones. Could this be the Eleanor?

### 255. Armed British merchant steamship MARY BAIRD
LOCATION:   50° 10′ 12″ N. 05° 43′ 42″ W.

The Mary Baird was a vessel of 1830 tons gross, was built in 1908 by A. G. Neptune, and had dimensions of 261·1 × 39·2 × 16·9.

On 18th May 1917, she sank after hitting a mine '2½ miles W by N from Pendeen Cove', with the loss of 7 lives.

The wreck most probably lies outside the 20 fathom line in around 150 feet of water—and in addition, the sea between the presumed wreck area and the mainland teems with very nasty races.

### 256. Unknown
LOCATION:   50° 09′ 06″ N. 05° 45′ 48″ W.

This is a fairly large wreck, first reported by the Escort Group No. 30 during World War Two. But this report only indicated that the wreck was there, with no other details.

At a later date another survey confirmed the position, adding that the wreck was lying 015° × 195°, at least 30 feet high and 142 feet in length.

Several years later, the Escort Group No. 9 confirmed the position yet again, gave the wreck as lying 015° × 195°, at least 20 feet high and 81 feet in length. Now, a wreck usually collapses quite quickly after a while, but the length disappears much more slowly, so it is possible that someone made a wrong reading somewhere—but that is only my opinion.

Like Wreck 255, this one lies beyond the 20 fathom line.

### 257. Unknown
LOCATION:   50° 08′ 24″ N. 05° 50′ 30″ W.

This is a very large wreck, in very deep water. It was first located in 1945. The survey ship worked out that the remains were 48 feet high and 400 feet in length, lying 060° × 240°. Big indeed. In fact it seemed so large that it was decided to check that the bump on the bottom was really man-made. To this effect the survey ship dropped a depth charge over the mound, and light oil was promptly given up. (This method was quite common with the less sophisticated methods of detection available then.)

### 258. Unknown
LOCATION:   50° 07′ 30″ N. 05° 50′ 18″ W.

This wreck is even larger than Wreck 257, which lies nearby. It was first located during World War Two, when it was reported as being 60 feet high and 400 feet in length. As with the previous wreck, a depth charge was dropped over the site, which gave up some light oil.

### 259. British cargo steamship DATETREE
LOCATION:   50° 07′ 14″ N. 05° 43′ 12″ W.

The Datetree was a vessel of 1995 tons gross, was built in 1914 by Antwerp Engineering Company, and had dimensions of 270·6 × 40·2 × 19·5 (last figures in depth, not draught). At the time of loss the vessel was either owned or managed by Howard Jones and King.

While on route from Barry to Brest with a cargo of 800 tons of coal, the Datetree ran aground on the Brisons, near Cape Cornwall, in dense fog. This was on 25th June 1914—she was not a year old. One newspaper report states that 'the cargo was jettisoned at the time of loss'. Obviously this only means *some* of the cargo.

Presumably the crew tried to lighten the load to get the vessel off the rocks.

The Brisons are a nasty group of rocks offshore between Cape Cornwall and Gribba Point. Relatively shallow on the east or mainland side, they drop into 80 feet of water to the west.

### 260. Unknown
LOCATION:    50° 04′ 40″ N. 05° 50′ 42″ W.

This is a fairly large wreck which was first located by the Escort Group No. 2 during World War Two. The position has since been confirmed. The remains are estimated to be some 36 feet high and 203 feet in length. This is another case where the first survey ship dropped a depth charge over the site, and oil was given off.

### 261. Cardiff tramp steamer BLUE JACKET
LOCATION:    50° 03′ 57″ N. 05° 44′ 42″ W.

This iron vessel was of 2090 tons gross, was built in 1883 by J. L. T. Thompson and Sons, and had dimensions of 283 × 37 × 24. The Blue Jacket was actually wrecked less than 50 yards from the main entrance to the Longships Lighthouse on 9th November 1898. As a result of this, another wreck is located nearby! The records show that on 9th February 1900, the tug Chase was lost off Land's End 'while working the wreck of the Blue Jacket'.

### 262. Unknown
LOCATION:    50° 03′ 27″ N. 05° 48′ 42″ W.

This wreck was first located by the Escort Group No. 9 during World War Two. The position has since been confirmed. The Group recorded that the wreck was 24 feet high and 133 feet in length, lying 017° × 197°. A depth charge was dropped and oil was given up.

### 263. British steam collier CITY OF CARDIFF
LOCATION:    50° 03′ 15″ N. 05° 41′ 45″ W.

This vessel was of 3089 tons gross, was built in 1906 by Ropner and Sons, and had dimensions of 330 × 48 × 22.

While on route from Le Havre to Cardiff, probably in ballast, she was caught in a gale and blown ashore at Nanjizel Bay near Land's End. The remains of a boiler show at low water springs in this area, and it is understood that this is the City of Cardiff.

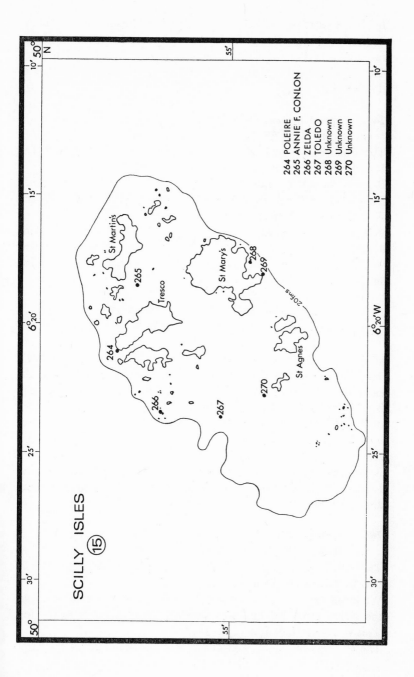

SCILLY ISLES ⑮

N

St Martins

Tresco

St Mary's

St Agnes

●265
264
●266
●267
●270
●268
●269

20 fms

264 POLEIRE
265 ANNIE F. CONLON
266 ZELDA
267 TOLEDO
268 Unknown
269 Unknown
270 Unknown

It almost certainly is, but the reason why I include it here is because I understand (and it is only a rumour) that some divers recently found a name plate on this wreck—and it did not say City of Cardiff. Does anyone have any positive identification of this wreck?

### 264. Cypriot ore carrier POLEIRE
LOCATION: 49° 57′ 57″ N. 06° 21′ 04″ W.

The Poleire, a vessel of 1599 tons gross, was grounded on The Kettel, north of Tresco, in dense fog, on 15th April 1970.

Reports by RNA Culdrose and St Athens indicate that the wreck lies east–west, the bows in 30 feet of water and the stern in 60 feet. A local salvage firm has removed the screw.

Not much of a mystery so far. However, the Poleire was carrying a cargo of zinc concentrate, which was not salvaged. Scientists would like to know if the concentrate is having any effect on life in the area. So if you're passing by . . .

### 265. American schooner ANNIE F. CONLON
LOCATION: 49° 57′ 30″ N. 06° 18′ 30″ W.

The Annie F. was carrying a cargo of oil casks when she was sunk by gunfire from a German submarine on 5th October 1917. The position of the wreck was originally well known because the oil casks were later salvaged. A Trinity House report of November 1920 states that the remains are 'about 100 yards north-west of Broad Ledge off St Martin's; there are three pieces of the wreck in a 200 yard area'.

Again, not much of a mystery. In fact I should not be surprised if the area is already dived on. But I have included it here because I understand that the Annie F. is of interest to ship historians, and there may be a few pieces left to collect.

### 266. Steamer ZELDA
LOCATION: 49° 56′ 50″ N. 06° 23′ 30″ W.

The Zelda was a vessel of 1300 tons gross, owned at the time of loss by Glynn and Company of Liverpool.

While on route from Liverpool to Palermo with a general cargo, the Zelda grounded and was wrecked on rocks in a heavy fog. This was on 16th or 18th April 1873.

The site was originally well known because virtually all the cargo was salvaged in an operation covering many weeks.

I am not too sure about the location now. A report in the Hydrographic Department, dated 1970, states that divers had located a wreck 'west of Bryher, on Maiden Bower, mostly broken up and lying north–south, the stern in 35 feet and the bows in 90 feet of water'. This is *presumed* to be the Zelda, but the divers brought up no positive identification.

### 267. British steamship TOLEDO

LOCATION:   49° 55′ 16″ N. 06° 23′ 36″ W.

The Toledo was a vessel of 2843 tons gross, with dimensions of 301 × 42 × 29.

While on route from Galveston to Rotterdam with a general cargo, she hit Steeple Rock on 20th August 1898, in thick fog, rolled over and sank.

For a while the masts of the wreck were considered a danger to navigation, so they were levelled with explosives. A more detailed account can be found in Volume 3 of *Cornish Shipwrecks* by Richard Larn (published by David and Charles).

A recent report dated 1972 states that a wreck has been found in the position given above, and it is *presumed* to be that of the Toledo. Can anyone verify this?

### 268. Unknown

LOCATION:   49° 54′ 30″ N. 06° 17′ 30″ W.

Is this a wreck? A report by RNS Culdrose dated 1966 stated: 'In this position we found two old Admiralty pattern type anchors —no time to investigate fully'. The position is just between Tolamn Point and Church Point, St Mary's, and should be worth a visit— if only for the anchors.

### 269. Unknown

LOCATION:   49° 54′ 10″ N. 06° 18′ 04″ W.

Another real mystery. All that is known is contained in a diver's report of 1971, which said: 'There is a wreck here, in the same position as the Minnehaha. A bell, dated 1864 or 1869, was recovered.'

A vessel named the Charles Maureaur did go down in this area around that date, but is it likely that she would have carried a bell of the same approximate year? It would be interesting to

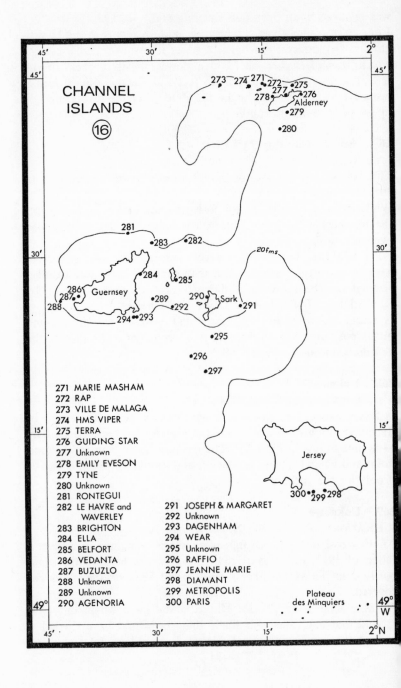

CHANNEL
ISLANDS
⑯

271 MARIE MASHAM
272 RAP
273 VILLE DE MALAGA
274 HMS VIPER
275 TERRA
276 GUIDING STAR
277 Unknown
278 EMILY EVESON
279 TYNE
280 Unknown
281 RONTEGUI
282 LE HAVRE and
    WAVERLEY
283 BRIGHTON
284 ELLA
285 BELFORT
286 VEDANTA
287 BUZUZLO
288 Unknown
289 Unknown
290 AGENORIA

291 JOSEPH & MARGARET
292 Unknown
293 DAGENHAM
294 WEAR
295 Unknown
296 RAFFIO
297 JEANNE MARIE
298 DIAMANT
299 METROPOLIS
300 PARIS

Guernsey

Sark

20 fms

Jersey

Plateau
des Minquiers

Alderney

locate the finders in case the bell presented some further information after cleaning.

## 270. Unknown

LOCATION: 49° 54' 07" N. 06° 22' 47" W.

A good one for the wreck detective. Ever since the turn of the century, Admiralty Charts have had the legend 'old wreck' next to a 'one fathom & shoal patch'. The point it refers to is called Old Wreck Rock. Everyone knows why it is called by that name, but no one seems to know for sure what the wreck—if there was one —is.

The position lies off Haycocks, north of the isle of Annet. It should make an interesting expedition.

## 271. German steamship MARIE MASHAM

LOCATION: 49° 44' 28" N. 02° 14' 38" W.

The Marie Masham was apparently a fairly large wreck, although I do not have any details—I suppose Lloyds could help. All that is known is that she was lost 'off Nannels' on 13th August 1907. There is a possibility that she went down outside the 20 fathom line, which is slightly to the north, but it is more likely that she was wrecked in the rather nasty group of rocks in this area.

## 272. Norwegian steamship RAP

LOCATION: 49° 44' 24" N. 02° 14' 31" W.

The records of the Hydrographic Department only state that the Rap was 'lost off Pierres des Butes on 11th June 1910'.

I have a little more than that—but not much. The Rap was built in 1882, and was on route from Newcastle to Gibraltar with a cargo of coal when, according to a copy of *The Times*, she 'went ashore to the east of Burhou, Alderney'. The captain apparently asked some boats to salvage some of the cargo—or perhaps he was trying to lighten the vessel in an attempt to get her afloat again—but she broke in two only a few hours later.

In fact the location given here should be very near that of the Marie Masham (Wreck 271), so the site is doubly worth a visit.

### 273. French steamship VILLE DE MALAGA

LOCATION: 49° 44′ 17″ N. 02° 20′ 34″ W.

This French vessel was of 1464 tons gross, and had dimensions of 240 × 34·1 × 15·1.

The exact site of—or even the reason for—the wreck is not known as far as I can tell. Records state that she was lost 'off Pommier Banks' on 14th August 1897, with the loss of 7 lives. Was this the entire crew? If not, someone must have survived to tell the tale.

Pommier Banks lie to the west of the Ortac Channel, and the surrounding water, while only about 16 feet deep in the immediate vicinity, soon drops down to 120 feet plus.

### 274. Destroyer HMS VIPER

LOCATION: 49° 44′ 14″ N. 02° 16′ 32″ W.

The Viper was of 440 tons *displacement*, was built in 1899 and had dimensions of 210 × 21 × 12·5. Armament consisted of one 12-pounder and five 6-pounder guns, and two torpedo tubes.

The vessel was wrecked, in thick fog, on 3rd August 1901. Three different reports of the wrecking were given in after the event, and they state that the wreck occurred on Runoquet Rock, Burhou Islands, and Bushon Islands. The last named is obviously misspelt—probably from handwriting intended to read Burhou. Runoquet is not on any of my charts, but it might well be the name of one of the rocks of the Burhou group.

This destroyer would be of particular interest to ship historians because she was the very first turbine engined destroyer ever built. It is recorded that the wreck has been sold to a Mrs M. Jean, a local resident. But this does not mean that the owner actually knows where the wreck is.

### 275. British steamship TERRA

LOCATION: 49° 44′ 11″ N. 02° 10′ 39″ W.

This was a vessel of 2801 tons gross, with dimensions of 314 × 40·5 × 20·1. The owner at the time of loss was the Vulcan Shipping Company of Glasgow.

While on route from Newcastle to Genoa with a cargo of coal she was lost 'on or near Groist Ledge or Grois Rocks', according to the Court of Inquiry that followed. *The Times*, however, was

94

more definite in saying 'wrecked on Chateau Letock Rocks'. This was on 11th June 1910.

At the subsequent investigation, it was shown that there was some negligence on the part of the captain, but he was allowed to retain his certificate. Study of the records of the inquiry might throw up some important information as to the location of the wreck.

### 276. GUIDING STAR
LOCATION: 49° 43′ 27″ N. 02° 09′ 30″ W.

I have only a few sparse reports on the Guiding Star. She was stranded on Gonah Rock, which is surrounded by relatively shallow water, in 1920. An early 1921 report stated that 'the vessel is fully submerged at half tide'. Another, late in 1921, said 'the wreck is now well broken up'.

The site is on the eastern side of Alderney, and should be easy of access. The remains, by now, will have been pounded to pieces by the sea, but there should be plenty of artifacts left.

### 277. Unknown
LOCATION: 49° 43′ 27″ N. 02° 11′ 32″ W.

Another shallow water wreck off Alderney, this one on the northern coast, in a bay sheltered from southerly winds.

This wreck was first reported in 1960, although the locals have probably known of it for a while because the frames dry at low water springs. It is marked 'Obstruction' on the latest charts, but it is a wreck. Despite its accessibility, which must mean that it has been dived on frequently, the name, as far as I know, is still a mystery.

### 278. Steamer EMILY EVESON
LOCATION: 49° 43′ 09″ N. 02° 13′ 29″ W.

This vessel was carrying a cargo of coal on 20th May 1922, when she was stranded on rocks, in dense fog, close to Fort Fourgis on the west side of Alderney, close to shore. Both sides were badly holed, so much so that coal was seen dropping out of them. Although I am assured that the exact site is now unknown, I find this difficult to believe. However, the remains might be broken up and difficult to find—but they will still be there. Or at least some of them will.

### 279. British steamship TYNE

LOCATION: 49° 42′ 00″ N. 02° 11′ 30″ W.

This vessel was of 647 tons gross, and was built in 1880.

While on route from Alderney to London with a cargo of granite, she struck Bonit Rock on 12th January 1912, and sank within three minutes—not surprising with a cargo like that.

The site is just off the north-east side of Alderney, and should not be too difficult to find—I should imagine somebody already has.

### 280. Unknown

LOCATION: 49° 40′ 34″ N. 02° 12′ 27″ W.

This wreck is an old one, even though it was first reported in 1966. This report stated that it was an 'old wooden ship'.

Several groups have dived on the site, but as far as I know the name of the vessel is still a mystery.

Some transit bearings are: easternmost tangent of Les Noires Putes, in line with the gap between easternmost two of Les Etaes, in line with La Roque Pendaute just open west of Qunard Lighthouse.

### 281. French steamer RONTEGUI

LOCATION: 49° 32′ 00″ N. 02° 33′ 00″ W.

This iron vessel was of 554 tons net, and was built in 1870.

While on route from Oran to Dunkirk with a cargo of iron ore and wine, she struck the Petite Rock, on the northern side of Guernsey, and foundered on 16th March 1880.

That, at least, is the story according to reports of the time. The trouble is, the name Petite Rock is not on any chart. It might be a locally used name, or one which is no longer used, or even a writing error. If you could find out where this 'Petite Rock' is, the Rontegui should not be far away. With a cargo like that she should have gone down pretty quickly.

### 282. Iron paddle steamer LA HAVRE
### Iron steamer WAVERLEY

LOCATION: 49° 31′ 17·5″ N. 02° 25′ 13″ W.

There are two wrecks here, both well documented, and as such not exactly a mystery. However, I have included them because at least one, the La Havre, is of immense historical interest because of the combination of age and type of vessel. Any items of this wreck would be worth a place in most maritime museums.

The La Havre was a Western Railways paddle steamer of 387 tons gross, and built at Blackwall in 1856 with dimensions of 184 × 24 × 14·5.

While on route with a general cargo, including mail, she was wrecked on Flat Bone Rock (another report says Platte Boue). Another report states that the La Havre was wrecked 'on the same rock as the Waverley'—which brings us to that vessel.

The Waverley was also a Western Railways steamer. She was of 593 tons gross, was built in 1868 and had dimensions of 222·2 × 26·8 × 13·5.

While on route from Southampton to St Peter Port, she was wrecked on 5th June 1873, two years before the La Havre. The reports of the wrecking vary somewhat. The generally accepted position is Flat Bone Rock, but other reports mention 'on Tautenay Rock and the head of the Small Russel', and 'on Pumps Rock, 3 miles from the Guernsey Coast'.

Going back to the La Havre, it is interesting to note that the alleged cause of the sinking was the fact that 'the beacons on the rock were obscured by fog'. This indicates that there are probably plenty of other wrecks around the rock.

### 283.  British steamer BRIGHTON
LOCATION:   49° 31′ 15″ N. 02° 30′ 00″ W.

This iron steamer, of 136 tons gross, and built in 1857, was owned by the London and South Western Railway.

While on route from Weymouth to Guernsey, she was stranded on Grand Braye Rock on 29th January 1887. All were saved, including the 23 passengers, but she later became a total wreck.

This site, incidentally, is extremely close to the 20 fathom line.

### 284.  Swedish wooden barque ELLA
LOCATION:   49° 28′ 30″ N. 02° 31′ 30″ W.

The Ella was a vessel of 421 tons gross, and was built in 1854.

While on route from Gothenburg to Liverpool, via Guernsey, with a cargo of pit props, she was stranded on Belgrave Rock on 11th January 1887, and became a total wreck.

The site is very close to shore, so I should imagine that someone has visited the remains. Or have they?

### 285.  French steamer BELFORT

LOCATION:  49° 28′ 00″ N. 02° 26′ 30″ W.

This iron steamer was of 491 tons gross, and was built in 1876. While on route from Bilbao to Dunkirk, with a cargo of iron ore, she was stranded on Selle Rock on 30th August 1887, and became a total loss.

The site of the wreck is on the south-east side of Herm, between the island itself and a group of rocks called Les Grands Bouillons. You would almost certainly have to charter or hire a boat from nearby Guernsey for an expedition, but it could be worth it.

### 286.  Sailing barge VEDANTA

LOCATION:  49° 26′ 40″ N. 02° 40′ 00″ W.

The only information I have on this is that the Vedanta was wrecked on Brayes Rock, Guernsey, on 11th February 1914.

The site is exposed to ferocious Atlantic weather, but is relatively sheltered from easterly winds. The area itself is rather shallow, with nasty rocks drying at low tide all around, so watch out if you use a boat for the visit.

### 287.  French steamer BUZUZLO

LOCATION:  49° 26′ 30″ N. 02° 40′ 33″ W.

The Buzuzlo was formerly called Weston.

All that is known is that the Buzuzlo was lost near Pezeris Bay in December 1896. One of her lifeboats was later washed ashore in Pezeris Bay; it had two occupants, both dead. This bay, as mentioned for the previous wreck, is rather shallow all over, and studded with rocks that touch the surface.

Where can the wreck be? It might be worthwhile reading reports of the finding of the lifeboat. If the occupants died from injuries, then it is possible that the location is not too far away. However, if they died from exposure, it is unlikely the vessel was wrecked in the bay itself. There are many groups of rocks—Les Trois Pères, Les Hannois, and Banc des Hannois—that could have claimed the Buzuzlo. And from any of these locations a straight drift to the east would have guided the lifeboat into Pezeris Bay.

### 288.  Unknown

LOCATION:  49° 26′ 22″ N. 02° 42′ 25″ W.

In 1911, a report to the Hydrographic Department stated that 'the wreckage of a small steamer lies at Le Maure Rock, near Hannois'. Nothing else has been reported since.

The general area, as with the two previous wrecks, is relatively shallow, which is the reason why survey ships have not visited the exact site. But for anyone in the Guernsey area, the location could be worth a visit.

### 289.  Unknown

LOCATION:  49° 26′ 24″ N. 02° 29′ 56″ W.

The position of this wreck has been confirmed several times. As the area was surveyed prior to 1942, when nothing was found, and in 1943, when it was, it can be assumed that the wreck is of 1942 vintage. But of course it is not certain that the first survey went over the exact site.

The remains are about 245 feet in length, 45 feet wide, and stand some 25 feet high—a big one indeed. Depths average around 85 feet, and the wreck lies 200° × 020°.

The bearing and distance is: from Doyles Column 062½° 1·59 miles, or; from Castle Breakwater Light 132½° 1·38 miles, or; from the beacon called Demie Femere, 252½° 9·45 cables.

### 290.  Schooner AGENORIA

LOCATION:  49° 26′ 24″ N. 02° 22′ 21″ W.

This is a World War One casualty, but I have no details other than that the Agenoria was wrecked near Platte Rock, on the west side of the island of Sark.

The site is close to shore, and I can vouch that the underwater visibility around Sark is something quite special when conditions are right. Anyway, if you do not find the Agenoria, this island is studded with wrecks. And to my knowledge the waters are rarely dived in.

### 291.  Brigantine JOSEPH AND MARGARET

LOCATION:  49° 25′ 33″ N. 02° 18′ 00″ W.

I have nothing more than the fact that the Joseph and Margaret vanished off Blanchard Rocks on 11th February 1887.

Blanchard Rocks lie to the east of the island of Sark. It is easy to find—there is a buoy and flashing light. Depths in the surrounding area average from 30 to 60 feet. However, the rocks are surrounded on all but the west side by the 20 fathom line.

I should think that the Blanchard Rocks rarely see divers, and because of this are worth a visit.

## 292. Unknown

LOCATION:  49° 25′ 34″ N. 02° 27′ 07″ W.

This wreck was first located in 1969. It lies at a depth of 115 feet, on a bed of shell and small stones in which it is well buried.

RN divers made a quick visit to the wreck during the survey, and guessed from the remains that it was a tug with two small barges alongside. Sounds like an interesting story.

The Decca position is: Red C 13·78. Purple B 74·61.

## 293. British steamship DAGENHAM

LOCATION:  49° 24′ 55″ N. 02° 32′ 10″ W.

The Dagenham was of 1466 tons gross, was built in 1907 by J. Crown & Sons, and had dimensions of 239·3 × 36 × 15·5. She was owned at the time of loss by Furness Whitby & Sons.

While on route from Newcastle to St Malmo with a cargo of coal, the Dagenham ran on to Grunes Rock (La Grune on the charts) which is off the south-east coast of Guernsey, or south of Herm. This was on 8th April 1909, and she became a total loss. At the time of the event, the sea was perfectly calm and it was daylight, so an inquiry was held.

The Court of Inquiry came to the conclusion that Captain Denyer steered too fine a course and neglected to take proper bearings of Les Hannois Lighthouse as it came into view, thereby causing the loss of the vessel, valued at £13,000.

When she first grounded, the Dagenham broke in two, the stern sinking immediately and the fore part remaining on the rocks for some time.

Depths in the area average some 90 feet. This location is very near that of Wreck 294.

## 294. British steamship WEAR

LOCATION:  49° 24′ 55″ N. 02° 32′ 10″ W.

This vessel was of 1076 tons gross, was built in 1905 by S. P. Austin & Sons, and had dimensions of 222·2 × 32·2 × 14·3. The owner at the time of loss was Witherington and Everett.

While on route from Newcastle to St Servian with a cargo of coal, she struck the Grunes Rock and foundered on 15th May 1910.

This wreck should be very near that of Wreck 293, so it would be worth searching the area for both of them.

## 295. Unknown

LOCATION: 49° 23' 08" N. 02° 21' 45" W.

This wreck was first located in 1960. Just about all that is known of it is that it resides in depths averaging 150 feet—much too deep for all but the very experienced divers.

## 296. Italian steamer RAFFIO

LOCATION: 49° 21' 30" N. 02° 24' 30" W.

I have no specifications of the Raffio, but if you do find the wreck —which sank off Sark on 6th May 1931—you should also find the wreck of the French steamer Jeanne Marie, which had previously sunk with a cargo of copper ore (Wreck 297).

Apparently, the Raffio was attempting to salvage the ore in the Jeanne Marie. According to *The Times*, 'Captain Laterule (of the Raffio) and 17 survivors landed at Guernsey. While attempting salvage, a 7 ton concrete dead man was being lowered over the side when the guy rope of the boom parted, and the boom swung out at right angles to the deck. The leverage tipped the Raffio over, and she turned and sank. The Raffio was equipped with the latest modern salvage equipment.'

I should think it virtually certain that such a valuable cargo as copper ore was eventually salvaged, although I have no record of this; mind you, the Raffio did salvage some. So it would seem likely that the Raffio will make the most interesting dive of the two. The main difficulty is the depth, which is all of 150 feet.

## 297. French steamer JEANNE MARIE

LOCATION: 49° 20' 15" N. 02° 22' 10" W.

The Jeanne Marie was a vessel of 2971 tons gross, with dimensions of 311·2 × 45·9 × 20·5.

While carrying a cargo of copper ore, she struck a mine and sank on 4th March 1918 in general depths of 150 feet.

Some of the cargo was salvaged by the Raffio (Wreck 296), but the Raffio sank nearby before the operations were complete.

## 298. Belgian steamship DIAMANT

LOCATION: 49° 10' 00" N. 02° 07' 00" W.

A large vessel of 7195 tons gross, the Diamant was originally owned by the John Cockerill Line, but at the time of loss she was under German control as the plunder of war.

She was wrecked on Pog's Nest Rock on 20th September 1942, and became a total loss. There is an unconfirmed report on the files of the Hydrographic Department that a Mr L. Mecham has obtained a letter of title to the wreck from John Cockerill. Even if this is true, it does not mean that Mr Mecham knows where the wreck is. Mind you, the area is pretty shallow, so it would not surprise me if several people know because this is off the south coast of Jersey, which is well dived.

### 299. Steamship METROPOLIS
LOCATION: 49° 09′ 47″ N. 02° 08′ 30″ W.

This wreck was first reported by Mr Titherington, a well-known diver in the Jersey area.

The report stated: 'There is a wreck at the base of Ruadiere Rock. The remains of the bows are 25 yards from the top of the rock on the lower shoulder of the main rock to the south. The engine is at the rock/gravel demarcation line, with the stern on the gravel bed. The iron screw is also visible, but there are no boilers, or anchors on the chain. There is 8 feet of water over the wreck at low water springs.'

From records, it is assumed that this is the wreck of the Metropolis, which sank at this location on 18th February 1961. It would be nice to have this confirmed, or otherwise.

### 300. Paddle steamer PARIS
LOCATION: 49° 09′ 44″ N. 02° 09′ 00″ W.

This is another wreck reported by Mr Titherington, this one in 1970.

He stated that the wreck 'is completely covered with gravel, only the boiler, engines and paddles show. The remains break up easily when touched. It is 7 cables from Normont Point Tower, or 6 cables from Sillett Beacon.'

The paddles, of course, give the clue, and it is presumed that this is the site of the paddle steamer Paris, which sank here on 28th July 1863.

# BIBLIOGRAPHY

# BIBLIOGRAPHY

Many books have been published on the subject of shipwrecks. Most of them recount the sinking of a wreck, or wrecks, as an interesting story. This, while of obvious appeal to those who are not interested primarily in wreck research, means that the serious student has to plough through a mountain of admittedly attractive prose to extract a few facts. However, such books are often invaluable for the comprehensive details of the various wrecks, and are included here, as are the ones which deal with statistics and are mainly for the keen wreck hunter. Also included are books which, while not directly aimed at the wreck enthusiast, contain occasional snippets of valuable information; for example, books about the activities of the lifeboats. Lifeboats are often the last witnesses to a particular sinking, and their records are of obvious interest and value.

*Shipwrecks Around Britain.* Leo Zanelli (Kaye and Ward 1970).
   A real guide for wreck enthusiasts. Contains precise locations of 400 wrecks around Britain with details of dimensions, tonnage and cargo where known, type and depth of sea bed, and any surveys that have been carried out.

*Sub-Aqua Guide.* Leo Zanelli (Prenbourne 1972).
   Pages 139–162 contain a Wreck List of many wrecks around Britain.

*The Wreck Detectives.* Kendall McDonald (Harrap 1972).
   Thirteen stories of wrecks around Britain which have been found and investigated by divers.

*Cornish Shipwrecks.* Richard Larn and Clive Carter (David and Charles 1969–71).
   This is the reference book for Cornwall. In three volumes, covering the North Coast, the South Coast, and the Isles of Scilly.

*Shipwrecks at Land's End.* Larn and Mills (Larn and Mills 1970). A 32-page booklet of pictures with captions.

*Cornish Shipwrecks.* Noall and Farr (Tor Mark). Another 32-page booklet mainly of wreck photographs with captions.

*Loss List of Grimsby Vessels.* David Boswell (Grimsby Public Libraries and Museum 1969). A wreck list, in chronological order of sinking, of vessels sunk in the Grimsby area between 1800–1960. The list contains several hundred entries.

*Wreck and Rescue* (D. Bradford Barton). This is a series of books, written with the co-operation of the Royal National Lifeboat Institution, which are standard histories of Britain's lifeboats. As such, they contain much of value for the wreck detective. Below are listed the volumes in print at the time of writing. The publishers eventually hope to produce an index.

> *Cornish Coast* (three volumes).
> *Bristol Channel* (two volumes).
> *Essex Coast.*
> *Devon Coast.*
> *Coast of Wales* (two volumes).
> *Irish Coast* (three volumes).
> *Dorset Coast.*
> *East Anglian Coast* (two volumes).

*Encyclopedia of American Shipwrecks.* Bruce D. Berman (Mariners Press 1972). A major work of research. Contains a list of 13,000 wreckings around the coast of the USA.

*Shipwrecks of the Royal Navy.* William O. S. Gilly (John W. Parker, several editions from 1857 onwards). Narratives of Royal Navy shipwrecks, and a list of vessels lost, from 1793 to 1857. Second-hand copies can be picked up fairly easily because this was a popular book and many were printed. Most of the information is from Admiralty records.

*The Wreck Hunters.* Roger Jefferis and Kendall McDonald (Harrap 1966).
Stories of wrecks around Britain which have been found and investigated by divers.

*Shipwrecks on the Isles of Scilly.* F. E. Gibson (Gibson 1967).
An excellent 84-page paperback containing a comprehensive list of wrecks around the Scillies, in chronological order. Full of excellent photographs.

*Back of the Wight.* Fred Mew (The County Press 1934 and 1951).
Stories of wreckings around the Isle of Wight, with an excellent wreck list in chronological order. The second edition, which contains additions, is the most informative.

*The Underwater Book.* K. McDonald (Pelham 1968).
Reports of underwater work done around Britain. Includes some wrecks.

*The Second Underwater Book.* K. McDonald (Pelham 1970).
Sequel to *The Underwater Book.*

*Diving Around Britain and Ireland.* Leo Zanelli (Aquaphone 1968).
Diving sites around Britain and Ireland, including wrecks.

*Notable Shipwrecks.* No author listed (Cassell 1898).
Many wreck stories from around the world.

*Shipwrecks and Adventures at Sea.* Committee of General Literature and Education (Society for Promoting Christian Knowledge 19th c.).
Wreck stories from all parts of the world.

*Shipwrecks and Disasters at Sea.* W. H. G. Kingston (Routledge 1973).
Wreck stories around the world.

*Heroes of the Goodwin Sands.* Rev. T. S. Treanor (Religious Tract Society 1892).
Some stories of the lifeboats during wreckings on the Goodwins. Some useful information.

*Famous Shipwrecks.* Frank H. Shaw (Elkin Mathews & Marrot, 1930).
The title is descriptive, the information world-wide.

*Great Lakes Shipwrecks and Survivals.* William Rattigan (Wm. B. Eerdmans 1960).
Spectacular shipwrecks of the Great Lakes of America and Canada.

*Cornish Shipwrecks.* Frank Strike (Strike 1965).
Stories of several shipwrecks off Cornwall.

*Sinkings, Salvages, and Shipwrecks.* Robert F. Burgess (American Heritage Press 1970).
Stories of shipwrecks around the world.

*Peril of the Sea.* J. G. Lockhart (Philip Allan 1924).
More wreck stories around the world.

*The Story of the Great Armada.* John Richard Hale (Thomas Nelson).
For Armada wreck hunters.

*Sea Toll of Our Time.* Hadfield (Witherby 1930).
A chronicle of maritime disaster in the 30 years prior to 1930.
Folding wreck chart showing the locations of 26 wrecks.

*Sunken Treasure.* Latil and Revoir 1962.
Sunken and raised treasure. Chart of the routes of the Spanish galleons. Translated from the French.

*Shipwrecks of North Wales.* I. W. Jones (David & Charles 1973).
A definitive work. 39 illustrations, 25 plates, 10 charts. Around 1000 wrecks.

*Birkenhead and its Surroundings.* H. K. Aspinall 1903.
Photos and drawings. 6 chapters on wrecks, early ferries and shipping.

*Twelve on the Beaufort Scale.* S. Rogers 1932.
Wrecks and founderings caused by storms. Illustrated.

*Sea Fights and Shipwrecks.* H. W. Baldwin 1955.
18 different tales around the world.

*Britain's Lifeboats.* Dawson 1923.
Lifeboats, wrecks, old prints, photographs, folding chart.

*Deep Sea Salvage.* White and Hadfield (Samson Low, Marston).
Notable salvage feats.

*The Cry from the Sea.* Rev. T. S. Treanor 1897.
Goodwin Sands and Deal lifeboat men and wrecks.

*Wreck-SOS.* A. C. Hardy (Crosby Lockwood 1944).
How wrecks are salvaged.

*Wonders of Salvage.* David Masters (Eyre & Spottiswoode 1944).
Title indicates content.

*When Ships Go Down.* David Masters (Eyre & Spottiswoode 1932).
Tales of salvage.

*S.O.S.* David Masters (Eyre & Spottiswoode 1937).
Wreck stories.

*Divers in Deep Seas.* David Masters (Eyre & Spottiswoode 1938).
Tales of salvage.

*The Golden Wreck.* A. McKee (Souvenir Press 1961).
The story of the sinking of the Royal Charter off North Wales.

*Twenty Years Under the Ocean.* H. J. Bruce (Stanley Paul, 1939).
Tales of salvage.

*Down to the Ships in the Sea.* Harry Grossett (Hutchinson, 1953).
Salvage tales of a helmet diver.

*Diving for Treasure.* Clay Blair (Arthur Barker 1960).
The discovery of an ancient wreck—the Matanzero—off the
coast of Mexico.

*The Elingamite and its Treasure.* Wade Doak (Hodder & Stoughton 1969).
The discovery of the Elingamite off New Zealand.

*The Vengeful Sea.* E. R. Snow (Alvin Redman 1957).
Tales of shipwrecks.

*Pieces of Eight.* Kip Wagner (Longmans 1966).
Recovering the riches of a lost Spanish treasure fleet off Florida.

*The Sea Surrenders.* Capt. W. R. Fell (Cassell 1960).
Tales of salvage by the Royal Navy.

*Finders Losers.* Jack Slack (Hutchinson 1968).
How a group of divers found a wreck and lost a treasure.

*Seventy Fathoms Deep.* D. Scott (Faber & Faber).
With the divers of the Italian salvage ship Artiglio.

*The Egypt's Gold.* D. Scott (Faber & Faber).
Sequel to the above book, *Raising the Egypt's Gold and Silver.*

*History under the Sea.* Alexander McKee (Hutchinson 1968).

*The Treasure of The Great Reef.* Arthur C. Clark (Arthur Barker 1964).
Treasure wreck off Ceylon.

# INDEX

# INDEX TO NAMED VESSELS

114

| NAME AND DATE OF SINKING | WRECK NO. | NAME AND DATE OF SINKING | WRECK NO. |
|---|---|---|---|
| Vasco. 1916 | 67 | Warnow. 1917 | 242 |
| Vedanta. 1914 | 286 | Waverley. 1873 | 282 |
| Veni. 1948 | 179 | Wear. 1910 | 294 |
| Ville de Malaga. 1897 | 273 | William Hanbury. 1942 | 195 |
| Viper, HMS. 1901 | 274 | | |
| Volunteer. 1865 | 129 | Young Fox. 1928 | 154 |
| Wapello. 1917 | 58 | Zelda. 1873 | 266 |